Spirit of Wit

He was the Spirit of Wit — and had such an Art in guilding his Failures, that it was hard not to love his Faults . . .

Nathaniel Lee, *The Princess of Cleves* (1681)

Spirit of Wit

RECONSIDERATIONS OF ROCHESTER

Edited by

Jeremy Treglown

Archon Books
Hamden, Connecticut
1982

© Basil Blackwell Publisher 1982

First published 1982

Archon Books, an imprint of
The Shoe String Press, Inc.
995 Sherman Avenue
Hamden, Connecticut 06514

Printed in Great Britain

British Library Cataloguing in Publication Data

Spirit of wit.
    1. Rochester, John Wilmot, *Earl of* — Criticism
and interpretation
    I. Treglown, Jeremy
    821'.4   PR3669.R2

ISBN   0 – 208 – 02012 – 8

Contents

Foreword

Voltaire said Rochester was a man of genius and a great poet.
Critics in the moralistic English tradition have been more
reticent: Johnson patronized him as a decadent amateur, Leavis
wrote him off, and many others who can't have been ignorant
of him have neglected him altogether. There have been
enthusiasts of course, as David Farley-Hills's invaluable
Rochester: The Critical Heritage makes clear: Hazlitt, for
example, wrote a few tantalizingly sharp sentences about him,
and since Goethe and Tennyson no one has been able to ignore
A Satyr against Reason and Mankind. Again, in recent years,
with the help of David M. Vieth's edition, a number of books
and articles about Rochester have appeared. But he is still
undervalued and under-represented, and the purpose of this
collection of essays, based on the tercentenary conference at
Wadham College, Oxford in 1980, is to make available new
assessments and new knowledge.

Three main approaches, inevitably overlapping, have been
adopted. First, there are attempts to characterize Rochester's
poetry as a whole, in terms of its preoccupations and style and
by comparison with the writing of his contemporaries and
precursors. Barbara Everett sees his work in the light of one of
his best, and best-known, poems, *Upon Nothing*, drawing out
the complex imaginative vitality that lies behind his denials and
mockeries. John Wilders discusses his important place in the

tradition of Metaphysical wit, taking issue with L.C. Knights's disparagement of Restoration poetry. Peter Porter, himself a lyric poet, places Rochester in a line of lyrical realism from classical poets, particularly Martial, to modern writers such as Wallace Stevens and John Ashbery. And in my own essay, I try to locate the distinct though elusive aspects of Rochester's tone and narrative style that unify his work.

The second approach concerns itself more with particular social, intellectual and ideological aspects of Rochester's life and writing. Basil Greenslade describes the special circumstances of his civil-war upbringing, suggesting their political significance and the pressures they are likely to have imposed on the young poet. David Trotter, focusing on a problematic passage in *A Satyr against Reason and Mankind*, demonstrates Rochester's close engagement in a current ideological battle with the King's chaplains, which had wide implications. And Sarah Wintle discusses his controversial attitudes to women, seeing them in the context of seventeenth-century writings and, particularly, of a contemporary shift in the balance of the sexes in sexual mores themselves.

A distinctive characteristic of Rochester is his responsiveness to other people's work—the degree to which he adapts, criticizes, plagiarizes, mocks and, less often, pays homage to other writers. Again, concentration on this quality overlaps with other approaches, but there is much to be learned from close attention to the way Rochester's writing interacts with his reading. Pat Rogers provides the first really close comparison between Rochester's innovative literary satire *An Allusion to Horace* and its Latin source, showing how even very subtle adjustments throw into relief the idiosyncrasies of the English poet. Finally, Raman Selden traces the vacillating relationship between Rochester and the contemporary dramatist Shadwell in a way that reminds us of another, social, aspect of his art.

One way of recognizing an outstanding writer is that he yields much to, indeed stimulates, very different approaches. It is a quality that appears in Rochester, as these essays show. They have all helped me, and I believe will help others, to read him better and to value him more highly.

J.T.

The Sense of Nothing

BARBARA EVERETT

❧❧❧

Rochester's general character as a poet is evident to any reader. He is a realist, his world bounded by the limits of King Charles II's court and the London that lay immediately beyond. If this makes his field seem narrow, then so it is—compared at any rate with the greater of his contemporaries: Milton, Dryden, even Bunyan, all live and write in a wider, larger world. But if, in turn, the relative thinness of Rochester's work is noticed as little as it is by any enjoying reader, this is because of the poet's compensating skills: the casual certainty that makes the elegance of his style, the extremity with which he goes to the limits of his vision.

It is from the balance of these opposing elements that Rochester's work gets its peculiar character. On the one hand there is the accepted commonplaceness of its content and milieu, the lack of preliminary with which the poet takes his place ('Well, sir, 'tis granted I said'—this or that) among the 'merry gang' as Marvell called them, Dryden's 'men of pleasant conversation . . . ambitious to distinguish themselves from the herd of gentlemen', or Pope's more lethal 'mob of gentlemen who wrote with ease'. Precisely because he so takes his place, there remains a border area of his work where editors still argue about who wrote what; and about how much, precisely, can be thought to function ironically—irony in itself being an index of that social commitment. But, on the other hand, the best of

1

Rochester's poems could have been written by no one else; just
as it is a fact that he was clearly not just *one* of the 'mob of
gentlemen' but himself a social legend in his own time and for
at least a century after. The particular nature of Rochester's
involvement in the social life of his time is perhaps a matter on
which biography has never placed the right kind of stress, or
from which it has never drawn conclusions useful enough for
the poetry. Those of the events in his life which we know
something about suggest how necessary it was to Rochester not
merely to be in the fashion but to excel in it, to transcend it
almost—to do a thing so well that the mode itself broke under
him, unrepeatable. It is impossible to draw any other conclusion
from the Alexander Bendo incident, in which the poet
impersonated a quack with high success. The affair is usually
treated as evidence of his obsessive acting talents. What is not
mentioned is that the trick had been played at least twice
before: once by Buckingham, then more recently by Rochester's
own friend Sedley. Acting a quack was in fact a fashion among
the Wits.[1]

What distinguished Rochester was the strange intensity of
his need not only to follow the fashion but to follow it to
breaking point—the *extremity*, one might say, of his world-
liness. That he had been (in youth) drunk for five years on end
is something he was eager to tell Burnet on his repentant death-
bed; and it is a fact that his final collapse followed on a sick
man's ride back home to Somerset from London where he had

---

[1] See V. de Sola Pinto, *Sir Charles Sedley 1639-1701* (1927), pp. 62-3; also p. 62,
note 5: 'The idea of masquerading as an itinerant quack always had a fascination
for the Restoration gallants.' Dr Anne Barton suggests to me that Ben Jonson's
story of his own disguise forms a possible precedent: 'he with ye consent of a
friend Cousened a lady, with whom he had made ane apointment to meet ane old
Astrologer jn the suburbs, which she Keeped & it was himself disguysed jn a
Longe Gowne & a whyte beard at the light of ⟨a⟩ Dimm burning Candle up jn a
litle Cabjnet reached unto by a Ledder.' (*Conversations with Drummond*, in *Ben
Jonson*, ed. C.H. Herford and P. and E. Simpson (1925-52), I, 141.)

returned with the King after insisting on attending the races at Newmarket. It is this quality of extremity that distinguishes Rochester's poems, balancing their realism and elegance. Or perhaps, in the end, bringing about the *im*balance that an original genius must consist in. For a work of art is recognized by its incapacity to be absorbed wholly by the society which produces it, and which it represents so admirably. Rochester's most social poems are very odd products indeed, but with an oddity that has nothing to do with eccentricity. This oddity—the oddity of art, not of social or psychological idiosyncrasy—is less easy to define than it is to illustrate, and I should like to illustrate it, as it were, from the life, taking an incident and using it as a kind of metaphor for Rochester's poetry; but the life I want to use is not, as it happens, Rochester's own, but his father's.

The elder Lord Wilmot, a general in Charles I's army and an adviser of the young King Charles II, is said to have been a brave man and a wit—as a companion of the King probably needed to be. He was made Earl of Rochester, the title his son inherited when he was only ten, for helping the King escape after the defeat at Worcester in 1651. At least, 'helping' is (again) what the history books say he did. Clearly the award of an earldom suggests that he did *something* for it: but the King himself almost implies, in the account of the flight which he dictated to Pepys thirty years later, in 1680, that it was *he* who helped *Wilmot* to escape after the battle, and this is a view not unsupported by contemporary witnesses. For it is clear that Wilmot complicated the flight in one particular way. Charles says: 'I could never get my Lord Wilmot to put on any disguise, he saying that he should look frightfully in it, and therefore did never put on any'.[2] This is one of the King's own footnotes to

[2] *The Boscobel Tracts,* ed. J. Hughes (1830), p. 151. See also Richard Ollard, *The Escape of Charles II* (1966).

his account, as though he found it an importantly lingering memory, even if he could not entirely fathom it. And the refusal of disguise certainly did affect the flight, enforcing Wilmot's travelling separately, either in front or well behind, keeping his court silks and laces well away from the strenuously walnut-stained and ostler-coated King, whose menial state of dress the recording Pepys—describing it in immense and awed detail—nearly faints to think about. Wilmot, on the other hand, condescended to one compromise only: he carried a hawk on his fist. He must have been, one cannot help reflecting, glad to see the back of it, when after six long weeks they reached the coast and embarked for the continent: where Wilmot was to die in exile seven years later, during the Interregnum, leaving his title to his ten year old son. But Rochester may have inherited from that necessarily little-known father more than the title and the estate, quite as much as he had from his mother, a powerfully dominating and able Puritan lady: and what precisely he inherited is reflected somewhere, perhaps, in that curious event which the King recorded.

Probably Wilmot was being funny—certainly his remark *is* funny, when one considers that to look 'frightfully', or at least to look unlike one's normal courtly self, is the whole purpose of disguise, especially when one is running for one's life pursued by troopers across the boggy English woodlands. And Charles's evident happiness in all the play-acting of this marvellous adventure—which he harked back to, wistfully, for over thirty years afterwards—might well have aroused an acerbic wit in a more battle-scarred companion. But the humour remains conjectural. What shines principally in Wilmot's remark is its quality of sheer 'face', its highly independent disobliging *panache* that yet operates within a narrow social context that gives that mocking word 'frightfully' its peculiar character. ('One would not, sure, be frightful when one's dead.') It is the very impassivity of the general's remark, our difficulty in knowing what precisely Wilmot was at (though there is no difficulty in seeing that he did what he wanted, in his easy way) that suggests its special social function. This is an occurrence of that highly English social phenomenon, the use of *manners* to get away with almost anything: for heroism, folly, intelligence, guile, whimsy or sheer blankness of mind may lurk beneath that recorded turn of phrase.

A sense, perhaps unconscious, of what social tone may serve for must have come quite naturally to the Cavalier courtier. But when the same sense occurs in the far more conscious Restoration wit of the son, it forms the great originality of his verse. For it is Rochester, perhaps, who invents *vers de société* in English. The act of translation places a radically new stress, it might be said, on the mere proposition, so that the poem is now written 'about' rather than 'from' society, with a new kind of inside-outness that helps to explain why Rochester should be also perhaps the first user of pure irony in English after Chaucer. The complexities latent in writing English *vers de société* are nicely suggested in a recent poem by Philip Larkin which takes the actual phrase for its title; one of his most undermining poems, what is undermined in it is basically the '*société*', and yet it is, for all that, a brilliantly 'social' piece of verse.

Another and more explicit case of this highly ambiguous social fidelity can be observed through the letters of Henry James, from the moment at which the young American writer sends back home, in the late 1870s, his impressions of the English social scene—

The people of this world seem to me for the most part nothing but *surface*, and sometimes—oh ye gods!—such desperately poor surface!

—to that, some twenty years later, at which James struggles patiently to explain to a correspondent less sympathetic than his family just what he had meant by the extraordinary art with which he had recently (in *The Awkward Age*) dealt in that world of 'surface':

> I had in view a certain special social (highly 'modern' and actual) London group and type and tone, which seemed to me to se prêter à merveille to an ironic—lightly and simply ironic!—treatment . . . with no going behind, no *telling about* the figures save by their own appearance and action and with explanations reduced to the explanation of everything by all the other things *in* the picture . . .[3]

Rochester himself would not have been caught making such 'explanations' at all: he was even further ensconced behind that social 'surface', that world of appearance and action which there was 'no *telling about*'. He inhabited, he half invented, that English social world where James was never much more than a wonderful lifelong tourist; which is why, perhaps, Rochester needed those compensating retreats to his country estates which were his equivalents to James's American nationality, his family background and his Puritan inheritance.

It is because of this very immersion and silence on Rochester's part that, despite all the differences of temperament and period and nationality, James's more self-conscious and detached reflections can be useful in suggesting some of the peculiarly ambiguous, confining conditions of a social art like Rochester's. There is an odd parallel, perhaps, between that famous Max Beerbohm cartoon which makes some sort of cool comment on the way in which the James of the *Sacred Fount* period did and

---

[3] *The Letters of Henry James,* ed. Percy Lubbock (1920), I, 67, 341.

did not 'belong', representing him as stooping to examine with horrified concern the mixed sexes of the pairs of shoes left to be cleaned overnight outside the bedroom doors of some hotel or house party—and a hostile aside on Rochester by a Victorian critic. Alluding to the anecdote of Rochester's having posted a footman in a sentinel's red coat and with a musket outside the doors of court ladies to watch the goings-on, the critic glosses it by saying that the poet 'for no earthly reason you can think of, set detectives to note him the indiscretions of the Court'.[4] Criticism ought perhaps to be better than this at thinking of earthly reasons.

For, if Rochester's verse transcends its own representativeness, this is by virtue of the way in which it goes, one might say, to the end of the road; the way in which his commitment to social forms was a manner of breaking those social forms. The story of his drunken destruction of the King's upward-pointing chronometer, and the apparent prudery of his for centuries unprintable reason for breaking it, is one of the best-known anecdotes that have survived him—and in the same way, even his most elegant verse often resounds with the crash of breaking glass; or where there is no crash, a startled reader will find himself glimpsing a void beneath the bright surface, a vacancy beneath the brilliant style.

As an example of this method of transcending the temporal mode, it is worth considering what happens to a Hobbesian idea of time in one of Rochester's best-known poems. In another of these often-repeated jottings that compose the legend of Rochester's life, Anthony à Wood remarks—thinking, perhaps, of the sensitive and well-read seventeen-year-old who first arrived at court with a tendency not only to blush but to stammer—that 'the Court . . . not only debauched him but

---

[4] G.S. Street, *Miniatures and Moods* (1893), p. 27; quoted in *Rochester: The Critical Heritage,* ed. David Farley-Hills (1972), p. 254.

made him a perfect *Hobbist*'.[5] Hobbes, whose *Elements of Law*
include the laws that

> Continually to be outgone is misery.
> Continually to outgo the next before is felicity.
> And to forsake the course is to die . . .

was certainly the philosopher of Charles's court, as he had
himself been the tutor of the King—as he was, in fact, the most
popular philosopher of the age in some cultural sense: we are
told that in the year after Rochester died 'the folly and nonsense
of meer mechanism' had passed to the very craftsmen, even the
labourers of the time, who were 'able to demonstrate out of
Leviathan . . . that all things come to pass by an eternal Chain
of natural Causes', and that human nature was a mere
machine.[6]

It is hardly surprising that Rochester committed himself to
this most fashionable system, which was also the most
imaginatively challenging of his time, having a hard self-
consistency not easy to refute. All the more striking is the
transmutation of these ideas within the medium of Rochester's
verse: within, for instance, his 'Love and Life'. This incorporates
the materialist and mechanistic doctrine of Hobbes that the
only *real* time is time present: 'The *present* only has a being in
Nature; things *past* have a being in the memory only, but
things *to come* have no being at all . . .'[7] But in Rochester's lyric
these ideas are *not* incorporated, but rather disembodied,
attenuated, made to float lightly in the emptiness of the 'flying
hours':

---

[5] Anthony à Wood, *Athenae Oxonienses* (1691), II, 489.
[6] Edward N. Hooker, 'Dryden and the Atoms of Epicurus', in *Essential Articles for the study of John Dryden,* ed. H.T. Swedenberg Jr. (1966), p. 241.
[7] Thomas Hobbes, *Leviathan*, ed. Michael Oakeshott (1946), p. 16.

All my past Life is mine no more,
  The flying hours are gone

.   .   .   .   .

The Time that is to come is not,
  How can it then be mine?

If everything in Hobbes is material and mechanical, then everything in the poem is immaterial and organic.

In part this is a simple question of what happens to all statements within the quasi-musical discipline of poetry, which part liberates ideas and part destroys them. 'When a thing is too stupid to be said, we sing it'; and conversely to sing a thing may be to make it sound stupid—or if not stupid, then released into a kind of radiant folly. It may be relevant that elsewhere Hobbes admits that he cannot explain music—'I confess that I know not for what reason one succession in tone and measure is more pleasant than another'—and this issue seems to be supported by Dryden's comment that the philosopher 'studied poetry as he did mathematics, when it was too late'. There appear to be conditions separating philosophy in modern periods from music and poetry, so that if they come together, in—say—the Metaphysicals, the result does not resemble Lucretius or Dante, but has a startled paradoxical self-undermining wit, as of a man who now knows that he is doing the impossible. In such verse, ideas get airborne, or at least stand on their heads. And Rochester's 'Love and Life' does have this Metaphysical wit; its title is borrowed from Cowley, and the whole poem's movement has a quality of strong fantasy, an extravagance in self-commital to paradox, perhaps learned from Donne, whom Rochester sometimes seems to know by heart.

But the change in Hobbesian doctrine in 'Love and Life' goes beyond the effect of what we may call either a 'musical' or a 'metaphysical' discipline. Nominally it is spoken by a libertine, a rake on principle, a man whose wholly selfish moral presuppositions followed hard upon Hobbesian cosmology and accepted the practical consequences of disbelief in past and future. But Rochester's libertine first translates philosophical maxims, words used as counters to win intellectual assent, into factors of human consciousness; and then, with a kind of sublime or idiot logic, extends that consciousness into a radical self-undercutting, an intelligence almost self-destructive. The conclusions of that intelligence might have surprised even Hobbes. For Rochester's libertine, having no past or future, has, in all honest logic, no present either: unless we give the name of a 'present' to the poem itself, which the poet, however 'courtly' or 'gentlemanly', speaks as out of an essential solitariness, in a surprise of realization rendered by the abrupt, lucid monosyllables, that seem to resonate in a void. 'All my past life is mine no more . . . How can it then be mine?'

One of the 'mob of gentlemen' here speaks with that peculiar lucidity which is the speech of the inward self, alone; and it is with a curiously chaste impersonality that the libertine watches the 'flying hours' carry his life away into a driftage as of dead leaves, of 'Dreams', 'Images', memory. When this same rakish lover turns at the end of the second stanza, in a beautifully located surprise, to hand over the poem to its audience and reader, the suddenly-invoked Phillis, his courtesy and gravity are hardly at all ironic; his 'Miracle', in fact, is one of those most undermining of word-plays, where a quiet literalism forestalls metaphor, irony grows serious and pretence turns real:

> If I, by Miracle, can be
> This live-long Minute true to thee
>   'Tis all that Heav'n allows.

The brilliance of this small poem, and what surely explains its great popularity and its anthology status both in the poet's time and in our own, is the way it converts a relatively sterile proposition from Hobbes into a potent human moment. The poem is a 'saying' that moves itself into action, becoming the fulfilment of the promise it half makes; its conclusion thus 'seals' the poem like a personal crest on a document now long crumbled away. Given that this hypothetical and contingent 'Phillis' is partly a mocking relic of past tradition, and partly some future dream, this ending makes of the lines a decisive handing over of the self to some unknown quantity, the 'present' being only a knowledge of what is unknown. And this sudden, ironic and yet generous self-offering is so circumspectly dealt with as to be able to suggest the perpetual existence of the self as in a void, created from moment to moment as a poem is from line to line. For the poet of 'Love and Life' has, by definition, nothing at all to call his own — neither past nor future, nor any present that he knows, beyond that 'Miracle' of the poem's live-long Minute. Neither a philosopher nor a libertine but something more like an equilibrist, the poet balances in the void, sustaining himself on nothing whatever.

I have been hoping to suggest that Rochester's poems may only safely be said to be representative of the Restoration period if that period is defined very cautiously. The 1660s and 1670s through which Rochester lived and which, in literary terms at least, he helped to create, were something of a cultural no man's land, a pause in time equally out of touch with the past and future, the medieval and the modern. It was an age in which writers began to inch themselves along again, with what Emily Dickinson would describe as 'that precarious gait/Men call Experience'. Rochester's best poems, in short, were probably all written in that decade after the Plague had seemed to empty

London, and the Fire to level it. They were written, moreover, for a court presided over by a penniless king back home from banishment and living carefully hand to mouth. The period which we name after its political Restoration has a reality not confined to its King and his court; but it is that court sphere which colours with an intensity beyond its apparent importance some of the best literature of the time. Similarly, though there were a number of different aspects of the world of that court, the one which features most vividly in writers of the period was that which the Marquis of Halifax (elder brother of Rochester's closest friend, and an even cleverer man, perhaps, than Rochester himself) was to call, in his well-known essay on the King, 'His Dissimulation'. In the drafts for his *History* Burnet had given this 'art of concealing' in the Restoration court a historical basis, deriving it from Charles's education at the hands of a Queen Mother determined that her sons should not display the (in the event) fatal unworldliness of their father. Whatever its source, this court dissimulation, evoked in Halifax's brilliant scattered phrases, suggests a kind of evasive darkness that we should perhaps see behind the sparkle of Rochester's court verse:

> Men compared Notes, and got Evidence . . . His Face . . . would sometimes tell Tales to a good Observer . . . At last it cometh to Smile for Smile, meaning nothing of either Side; without any kind of Effect; mere Drawing-room Compliments . . . there was less Signification in those Things than at first was thought . . . He would slide from an asking Face, and could guess very well . . . It was a kind of implied bargain.[8]

[8] Gilbert Burnet, MS draft of *The History of His own Time,* printed as an Appendix to Ranke's *History of England principally in the Seventeenth Century* (1875), VI, 78; and Halifax, *A Character of King Charles the Second* (1750), pp. 15-46.

It was for this world of 'Smile for Smile, meaning nothing of either Side', that Rochester's love poems were written; his Satires are 'Notes', 'Evidences', telling 'Tales to a good Observer'. To describe his verse as a construct from a world of surfaces implies that it is always close to irony; but the concept of irony can only be used cautiously of Rochester. For since its Socratic origins true irony has always served some polemic purpose — its 'lies' have always functioned to make clearer some truth. Rochester's poems often have a highly ironic sound, but something like a total lack of any provable intention (or even tone), except possibly the intention of hollowing out the surface they so finely construct. Apart from this latent sense of void, there is no form of what James called 'telling about', 'going behind': only the 'explanation' by 'all the other things *in* the picture'. Rather than by a smoothness so excessive as to make us defensive (as in Swiftian irony), Rochester's poems show intent by minute flaws in that smooth surface, by local shocks and coruscations of wit. Even where Rochester's tone seems cool, sweet and safe, his wit leaps to the surface in striking, even dangerous, disjunctions of language which locally fracture the style, like the minute cracks that beautify crackleware ceramics. An apparently 'polite' poem that addresses its subject as a 'Fair nasty nymph' (as does 'By all love's soft, yet mighty powers') is not going to leave quite where it was a socially-orientated 'fair' sex that relies on its unfair fairness of face to get away with murder; nor does a poem that goes on to advise in the name of hygiene a more 'cleanly sinning' leave either hygiene, or sinning, quite where it was before. Swift's famous letter to a young woman approaching matrimony which primarily advises her to wash often and thoroughly is possibly sensible but not funny in any human way, because some degree of animus towards the female makes itself plain in the intemperate style of a man who is for good or bad never a pure ironist; similarly all the smoothness of even the Modest Proposer only enforces what any reader instinctively knows, that eating people is wrong. Rochester's equally profane and good-taste-violating poem on the 'Fair nasty nymph' is more purely ironic than Swift's letter because it voices no animus at all against women (I think it highly unlikely that the poet had any)—it voices nothing: it merely sets out the flaw in the china in the cool crack about the 'Fair nasty nymph'. Bodies being as they are, it is the social insistence on 'fairness' that is the thoroughly 'nasty' thing.

In very much the same way, but with a more expansively indecorous decorum, the better-known outrageously-ending lines that tell us how 'Fair *Cloris* in a Pig-stye lay' make it their business to flesh out the discrepancies between that 'Fair' and that 'Pig-stye'. But they do no more — they do not satirize; they leave both reader and Chloris 'Innocent and pleased', with their illusions in place even if not quite intact. Chloris ends happy with her fantasy of lust and her virginity both unviolated; the reader ends happy in the belief that pastoral tells him something true about life or love; everything in the pig-sty is lovely. The power of this poem, compared with that about the 'Fair nasty nymph', is the greater degree of poetic acceptance of the mode proposed, the triumphant, non-committal accomplishment of this vacuous, self-deceiving, dishonestly erotic pastoral. How good an actor Rochester really was is unclear—certainly he sometimes loathed whatever he meant by the image of 'this gawdy guilded Stage'; but he was perfect at assuming the pose of a certain verbal style. Thus the charm of the very popular 'Ancient Person of my Heart' is its embodiment of the innocence of tone and terrible social polish that make the deb an evidently unchanging type over several centuries of English social life. The pronunciation of the time brings together in an assonance words as discrepant as the frigidly social 'Ancient Person' ('Parson') and the boldly intimate 'Heart': the comical insistence of this paradoxical refrain—'Ancient *Person* of my *Heart*'—embodies a social type on the page, as elegant and peremptory as a pedigree cat.

That refrain from the 'Song of a Young Lady' makes relevant here an even more minute detail. In citing 'Ancient Person of my Heart' (with its capital P, capital H), as in most other quotations from Rochester's poems up to this point, I have deliberately used Vivian de Sola Pinto's Muses' Library text (Routledge and Kegan Paul, 1952, second edition 1964), which is now to some degree superseded by David M. Vieth's scholarly modernized edition (Yale University Press, 1968). Vieth modernizes because, as he rightly argues, there is no bibliographical authority for any of the Restoration editions of the poet. But this is helpful proof of the simple fact that, where literature is concerned, bibliography is frequently (like patriotism) not enough. The primary need in presenting a poet is not to obscure his tone; and certain of Rochester's poems are so social in tone as to profit from the retention of that Restoration and Augustan habit of visual literacy, the capitalization of important nouns. Thus, Vieth's able but toneless text renders meditative and inward a poem like 'Upon his Leaving his Mistress', a part of whose flagrant virtue it is to give the whole of social life the look of an open secret, a network of called passwords in a war, a surface of nods and becks which there is no 'going behind, no *telling about*':

> 'Tis not that I'm weary grown
> Of being yours, and yours alone:
> But with what Face can I incline,
> To damn you to be only mine?
> You, who some kinder Pow'r did fashion, ⎞
> By merit, and by inclination,   ⎬
> The Joy at least of a whole Nation.   ⎠

The first word the Muses' Library edition follows its 1680 text in capitalizing is the third-line 'Face'; the next in this stanza is 'Pow'r'. All the delicate contradictions of a lover's psychology, which the poem also manages to hint at, the ironies of a Petrarchan self-abasement in the sensitive lover's soul, are shouldered back behind and yet somehow expressed by the heightened capitalized forms of social observances, the agreement that socially it is 'Face' not feeling that matters, it is 'Pow'r' not love that governs ('continually to outgo the next before is felicity'); and in such a context to give or take fidelity is hardly a saving grace—it is to '*damn* you to be only mine'.

Rochester can write tenderer, more inward poems than this, such as justify Vieth's modernized reading of the poet. One of these more tender poems offers a stylistic detail as interesting as Rochester's use of capital letters: a rhythmic effect that speaks to the ear, as the capitals speak first or primarily to the eye. In each of the two, apparently highly conventional, stanzas of 'My dear Mistress has a Heart', the last foot of each of its four-footed lines is, in lines 2, 4, 6 and 8, a trochee ('gave me... enslave me . . . wander . . . asunder'); but lines 1, 3, 5 and 7 truncate their last foot by a syllable, so that 'My dear Mistress has a *Heart*' (not an ankle or an elbow). The result of this delicately asymmetrical scansion is that every line ends with what sounds like an unexplained falter, the odd lines because they have one syllable too few, the even because they have one too many. With a striking technical mastery, this effect of varying but inevitable falter, like a flaw in nature or an irony in the mind or what medicine calls a shadow behind the heart, is repeated conclusively in the structure of the whole; for the sense of the poem's first eight-lined stanza and then its succeeding six lines swells to a climax of feeling, of certainty, that is suddenly undercut by a kind of 'rhyme' the reader had not expected, the repetition at the end of the second verse of the last two lines of the first, a *reprise* like a stammer that turns the whole poem into an echo of its sustaining and yet faltering pairs of lines. And yet again, that falter finally does not seem to matter, because where the first time its rhyme-word 'asunder' occurred, it only half-rhymed with 'wander', here in the repetition it comes to rhyme with 'wonder', so the poem is after all strangely complete.

If 'My dear Mistress has a Heart' is touching and troubling in a way we do not necessarily expect a conventional Restoration lyric to be (so that Victorian critics used to compare it with Burns), the cause is a quality not often found in Restoration poems: its power of latency, its character of reserve. The blank general words with their capitals—'Heart', 'Constancy', 'Joys', 'Mankind'—are a fine hard surface under which (we delusively feel) the real life of the poem goes on; but we feel that real life at the point of breakage, where the poem falters for an instant and then carries on—where we see the surface as *only* surface, with perhaps vacancy beneath. But for this there are no 'explanations', there is 'no going behind'.

In all these poems, minute technical details—what one might call flaws of the surface—speak of conditions that one cannot consider in a merely 'technical' way. All Rochester's most potent and idiosyncratic lyrics develop this sense of 'flaw' into a condition of discrepancy that almost breaks apart the convention he appears to be working within—almost, but not quite: the result is never true burlesque, only a kind of agitation below the social surface. That agitation, or submerged quality of personal apprehension, can render the actual treatment of a conventional subject quite unlike what a reader might expect it to be. It might be said, for instance, that Rochester approaches the question of the physical in love as a libertine, with a frank and cynical 'realism'. That he has realism is true, but to say so may imply a quality of apprehension quite different from what

we actually find. To say that in 'The Fall' Rochester portrays
Adam and Eve as a pair of cool libertines caught between the
acts is to predicate a poem that has little in common with what
he actually wrote:

> Naked, beneath cool Shades, they lay,
> Enjoyment waited on Desire:
> Each Member did their Wills obey,
> Nor could a Wish set Pleasure higher.

The plangency of this comes partly from that negative, 'Nor
could', a little like Milton's 'Not that fair field of Enna'. But
what is even more striking is the absence of the sensuous, of
which the 'puritan' Milton's Adam and Eve in Paradise have far
more. When Poussin paints Adam and Eve in Paradise he gives
them, over their naked bodies, a hair-style comically close to
the great wigs of Louis's court, as though to his mind certain
aspects of dress can't be taken off even in Paradise, but are
generic to the human estate. Rochester, another court artist,
seems to be driven by a comparable yet reversed impulse. It is as
if, in order to undress his fallen couple, to get them back
towards whatever innocence once meant, *he* has to take off
their very bodies, which in this poem are dissolving towards the
Platonic condition of shadowy Idea, under trees so abstract as
to have grown mere generic 'Shades', dark reflections of
themselves, in an experience so reversed as to be only the
negative opposite of that dulled satiety which is the one happiness
we know. In Rochester's Paradise, 'Enjoyment waited', in a
past and future defended from the satisfactions of the horrible
present.

If this seems a strained reading of that strange abstract
stanza, it should be said that it is only consonant with the poet's
representation of physical existence throughout his work: all

Rochester's lovers are portrayed, at their most intense, like his Adam and Eve. If these first parents are abstracts, then the poet's typical lovers are simply ghosts, haunting a period of time never 'Now' but only a reflex of past and future. The manner of these poems will make a reader expect an art as of an expert social photographer catching smiling and solid persons in the bright light of the moment: but when looked at hard, these results are all negative. The speaker of 'Absent from thee', whose 'Fantastic Mind' desires only *not* to be a 'straying Fool', makes it his hope, not that he will be true, but that he will betray love *enough*—that he will tie a tight enough knot of punished infidelity to hold himself steady in: as steady as the poem is held by the syntactic knot of the line which sums up the only available alternative of fidelity—

> To wish all Day, all Night to Mourn.

'An Age, in her Embraces past' starts its vagrancies by letting the reader down from the expected summer's night which its erotic context suggests, into its actual 'Winter's Day' of love: a chilly actuality as mistily indecorous to our conventions of love as are the divergencies of the poem's chief character, a Shade of Soul that wanders ghostlily through the poem. Its path is indicated by a ramifying grammar—

> When absent from her Eyes;
> That feed my Love, which is my Soul,
> It languishes and dyes . . .

—that becomes a fragmented style from which even the poet dissociates himself contemptuously ('Love-sick Fancy'), thus disintegrating the medium still further. The poem at last rests for its stability on one conclusion only, that 'expiring' truth attained in 'Absent from thee'; here it takes the form of the stoical 'Pain can ne'er deceive', the belief that jealousy at least provides

> Proof 'twixt her and me,
> We love, and do not dream.

The time scheme proposed in this poem comes to rest, not on present moment, but on that shadowy past and future evoked in its last stanza's re-echoing rhymes, 'when past' and 'at last'. It would seem a mistake to write down this lack of the libertine art of present enjoyment to a mere bad mood of love, a passing depression. For this same insubstantial medium may be found in poems that cannot be written off as court lyrics of love. One of Rochester's strongest short poems, 'The Maim'd Debauchee', takes as surface (without quite burlesquing it) the graver heroic style of the period, and its vision extends as wide as state affairs: but it is a fact that its perspective on war and politics is identical with that of the lyrics on love. Immediately beneath the grave, powerful surface, all is a resonant dissolution:

> Shou'd some brave Youth (worth being drunk) prove
>   nice,
>   And from his fair inviter meanly shrink,
> Twould please the Ghost of my departed Vice,
>   If, at my Counsel, He repent and drink.

That the warrior of love here becomes a Ghost of Vice fits the peculiar decorum of the poem, for its situation offers the temporal vertigo of a man who lightens the miseries of present love by toughening himself with the reminder of the prospects of future impotency—the future pleasure, that is, of remembering a then past potency. The fragile, hardly Socratic, self-knowing wisdom which its last two syllables tender ('be wise') is something like the knowledge that human beings love, or lust for power, in order to enjoy looking forward to the pleasure of looking back at the pain of having suffered. It moves in fact from

> My Pains at last some respite shall afford . . .

to:

> Past Joys have more than paid what I endure.

The brute strength of these factual-sounding lines has to be balanced against the shadowy non-existence they record. The poem celebrates fulfilments never more than ostensible. And its title, 'The Maim'd'—or, as Vieth reads, 'Disabled'— 'Debauchee', compacts into a phrase the theme of impotency or emptiness below the surface of an extreme worldly experience.

This theme, brilliantly embodied in the matter of the poem, is oddly reflected too in one specific detail. I am still quoting here from the Muses' Library text of the poems; but in that edition, this poem's climactic stanza will not be found in the text, only doubtfully added to the notes at the back of the book. And even there, it is to be read only in the more decent version which the 1680 text printed, and which Vieth rejects for one hardly printable until a decade or so ago. Thus, earlier versions, extending over nearly three centuries, all give the poem as it were a hole in the page, a void between the lines. The editorial problem, in fact, which begins with a matter as simple as Rochester's use of the notorious four-letter word, properly considered takes us right to the centre of the whole question of his aesthetic purpose, as expressed in the characteristic abstract violence of his style. For an art that so brilliantly and customarily brings together fact and fantasy, the surface and the void, also brings together with particular point the elegant and the obscene. For in obscenity, in the words unprintable—except in pirated editions—even in Rochester's time, the extreme of verbal and emotional nothingness is reached. Whatever the changing proprieties in an age, an obscenity is a non-word, a hole in the page—a betrayal of human sense and meaning to mere grunting phatic gesture.

It is clear, I think, that Rochester, who is sometimes misnamed a pornographic poet, wrote as a man capable of thinking of his obscenities in precisely this way—with the eye and ear of the sensitive man who once came to court not merely blushing but stammering, finding certain things unsayable. Consider the missing stanza from 'The Maim'd Debauchee':

> Nor shall our *Love-fits Cloris* be forgot,
>   When each the well-look'd *Link-Boy* strove t'enjoy
> And the best Kiss, was the deciding *Lot*,
>   Whether the *Boy* us'd you, or I the *Boy*.

It could hardly be said that this gets worse when Vieth reads,

> Whether the boy fucked you, or I the boy . . .

In fact a strong case could be made for feeling that the verse undoubtedly gets better in the more brutal transposition. For that specific, end of the road, last-ditch verbal shock both embodies and in some curious way resolves the other much larger shock which the poem is about: which it is both about, and bespeaks in everything we mean when we gesture vaguely towards its 'mock heroic' or burlesque manner.

A more recent poem, one of Philip Larkin's, mentions the 'long perspectives / Open at each instant of our lives', meaning the deracinating shocks time brings to those whose element is said to be the temporal; and Rochester's 'obscene' stanza provides this among other shocks. It brings to a culmination, just before the end of the poem, everything *pastiche* in it up to that point: in an imitation of 'antiquity' whose soft delicate indelicate procedure has hardly been improved on in three hundred years of translation, imitation, pastiche and burlesque, up to and even including Pound's reversals and repetitions of a whole century of phoney classicism. Rochester's stanza aches with an almost Virgilian sense of distance, the yearning both of and for the classical, since all epic from Homer on looks back to an earlier innocence only surviving in an epic lumber of weapons, feasts, ships, the nicknames of gods and the code of poets. That loaded long-perspectived classic sense of life in time Rochester reaches back for and wraps around, not a battle or great feast but a memory of private pleasure; and that memory and that pleasure capsize the great mood, bring it down to a ground-bass of simple wordless obscenity. This last line is, in its way, perhaps tender, perhaps funny; it also shows reality dissolving, chaos and promiscuity taking over, and sheer nothingness opening all around.

The self-defeating lordly art of that 'unprintable' final line is generic to Rochester's work, which offers many parallels— though not, of course, in such older texts as the Muses' Library, in which a couplet or a whole poem will become that 'hole in the page': as where the poet, skating on the thin ice of obscenity, has fallen in. In all of them Rochester devotes his elaborate talent to capturing both phonetic and semantic nullity: as when he settles the scope of his monarch's affections with a noise as of a mud bath, in 'Love he loves, for he loves fucking much'; or, leaving his club or coffee house one evening, looks back, as it might be down to the bottom of a well, to see and hear the *Symposium* reduced to the sound of frogs—

> Much wine had passed, with grave discourse
> Of who fucks who and who does worse . . .

This reductiveness and this nullity are in fact the heart of the matter, for Rochester can when decorum demands maintain the same brutal art of monosyllables without the aid of obscenity, as when Artemisia gives us the whole Art of Love in wondering whether

> The old ones last, and who and who's together.

Similarly, the *Satire against Mankind* says the last word when it paraphrases the whole Hobbesian dance of human society as

> *Man* undoes *Man*, to do himself no good

—an extraordinary complexity of sonic monotony, a concrete music of fallen nature.

To observe the peculiar artistry of Rochester's single-lined brutalities is to understand more clearly what he is doing in whole poems like the extraordinary complex of finesse and unrepeatability, *A Ramble in St James's Park*, whose *Symposium*-like opening pair of lines I have just quoted (from Vieth's edition). The poem is a vision of the social scene as a violent phantasm, with the darkness of night-time London showing through it. Its poised yet perhaps three-quarters-mad speaker has been betrayed by the 'infinitely vile, when fair' Corinna, taking turns with three young blades (a Whitehall gadabout, a Gray's Inn wit, and a Lady's Eldest Son) who may well embody the world, the flesh, and the devil in person; and what maddens the poet to near screaming-point is that this semi-goddess has sold him *for nothing*, as exercise of mere preference of change for change's sake, fashion in love; a preference which therefore brings the speaker in all logic to recognize his equal guilt in similarly loving a mere nothing, a mere love object, a figment of imagination. In self-punishment as much as revenge he curses her with the fate logic demands: she shall 'go mad for the north wind . . . and perish in a wild despair'.

The *Ramble*'s savage, dangerous, yet obscurely innocent fantasy—innocent from the sensed rectitude which its upside-down fury violates, the contained and quashed romantic idealism without which we could not (I think) laugh at that wilfully frightful ending—epitomizes much of what Rochester does in his elegant and obscene writings. If one says 'much' rather than 'all', this is because the violently sustained grossness of the *Ramble*, its comic extravagance or fantasy of wildly pained love, unbalances that poise which the poet more usually maintains. A more representative art may be found in a slighter poem, in the delicate brilliance of the translated 'Upon Drinking in a Bowl'. This poem is from Ronsard's version of the Anacreontic 'Cup' lines. But Rochester's final effect is radically unlike the almost Jonsonian directness Ronsard keeps to here. Its difference will illustrate well enough—better in fact, than the *Ramble*—that art by which Rochester will place obscenity up against a brilliant social surface.

For the poet makes two mutually opposed departures from Ronsard. Taking a hint from Cowley's version of this much translated poem, Rochester gives it a vein of controlled fantasy that Ronsard knows nothing of: he replaces the French poet's sober directions by allowing the poem to mime before us the shaping of the cup, to call forth to the imagination the 'contrivance' and 'Skill' of its 'trimming', the chaste feel of it to the mind as it is 'Damasked . . . round with gold'. Fantasy begins to build on the simpler sensuousness of 'Damask': the 'swelling Brim' holds an almost Mallarméan vision of imagined toasts swimming on the 'delicious Lake, / Like Ships at Sea'; and on this image, the poem flashes through each stanza scenes of War, of the Planets, of a Vine, each perceived only to be rejected. The poem grows and solidifies as the imagined cup, an exquisitely 'holding' structure, is turned before us in an imagined hand. With the sixth stanza, quietly, this whole beautiful structure is tossed away, like a wineglass thrown over the shoulder. Building on a mere hint offered by Ronsard, who introduces a vulgarism (*'Trogne'*, 'mug' or 'phiz', for Bacchus's face), Rochester closes:

> *Cupid* and *Bacchus* my Saints are;
>   May Drink and Love still reign:
> With Wine I wash away my Cares,
>   And then to Love again.

In this last line, where the more seemly Muses' Library text reads 'Love', Vieth follows the 1680 text and prints a cruder monosyllable, mockingly alliterating with 'Cares'. This obscenity must be, I think, what Rochester wrote. He has given this exquisite but shocking small poem a wholly original structure, necessitating two opposed poles: the one creating in fantasy an extremity of imagining; the other with one casually dropped word shattering everything that has gone before. The final dynamic effect of the poem is not unlike the extraordinary structure which Milton's bad angels erect in hell: a brilliant energy of human creation, teetering over a void.

Rochester's biographers have noted that in his last years—his early thirties—his reading turned to history, philosophy and politics; and they have surmised on that basis that had he lived he might have given more time to the public affairs he had

profoundly despised earlier. In something of the same spirit
Robert Parsons implies that on his death-bed Rochester looked
forward to the writing of sacred poetry. Both prospects seem
unlikely. Both seem, moreover, to be associated with the kind
of anxiety that impels even his best critics (like, for instance,
David Farley-Hills in his admirable study) to overstress the
'positive' aspects of his work, either in the direction of making
much of the philosophical importance of his ideas, or of
underlining the exciting fictiveness of the more substantial
poems—of finding in them even the three-dimensionality of
the novelist. Both ventures risk distorting the real aesthetic
quality of Rochester's poetry. A moment's consideration of
some of the couplet poems will show how little truly 'fictive'
they are, how little they rest within the play of psychological
and social relationships.

Rochester's more overtly satirical writing makes it seem odd
that there is still any question as to why he chose Timon as a
persona. Shakespeare's character took the covers off the dishes
at his banquet to show, beneath, nothing but spangles and
warm water; and he looked forward to his removal from the
great social scene with the words

> My long sickness
> Of health and living now begins to mend
> And nothing brings me all things.

Of *A Letter from Artemisia in the Town to Cloe in the Country*
one might say that all things bring us nothing.[9] Some recent
critics regard this as Rochester's best poem, and the quality
most admired is its fictive density of substance, its moral

---

[9] I quote the Muses' Library title and text for this poem, while changing the
spelling of the name to Vieth's *Artemisia*, for reasons suggested in my discussion
of the name's possible source.

relativism. This admiration is responding to something true in the poem which explains its sheer entertainingness; but it is a dangerous admiration that overlooks an essential element of structure. 'Dear *Artemisia*! Poetry's a Snare': and this poem is as reductive, as self-underminingly self-consuming as anything Rochester ever wrote, the seductive promise of whole Decamerons of future stories with which it ends as unaccomplished and unaccomplishable as those 'Promises' and 'Vows' which end 'Upon Nothing': for Rochester was not a man who wrote the same poem twice. And it is an unalterable condition of the poetic form that, unlike drama or the novel, poetry has no free-standing voice, each persona must be taken responsibility for by the poet — who was, in this case, as peculiarly well known to the audience for whom he wrote for his masculine gender as for his aristocratic standing. Rochester never, that is to say, writes like a woman, only like a man writing like a woman, and carefully selecting only such female attributes as may solidify the equation latent in the opening that women are to men as the individual man of wit is to the rest of society. For, as Rochester says elsewhere,

> *Witts* are treated just like common *Whores*,
> First they're enjoy'd, and then kickt out of *Doores* . . .
> *Women* and *Men* of *Wit*, are dang'rous Tools,
> And ever fatal to admiring *Fools*.
> Pleasure allures, and when the *Fopps* escape,
> 'Tis not that they're belov'd, but fortunate,
> And therefore what they fear, at last they hate.[10]

[10] In the last line of this passage from the *Satire against Mankind*, Pinto follows the 1680 text in reading 'And therefore what they fear, at least they hate'. John Hayward, in his Nonesuch Press edition (1926), reads 'And therefore what they fear, at heart they hate'. I have silently altered the Muses' Library text here to 'last', a reading which I propose as possibly underlying the erroneous *least*; in literary terms, the conclusive ring of 'at last they hate' is both more Rochesterian and more generally Augustan.

From the beginning we hear Artemisia, for all the brilliance of the impersonation, as Rochester's voice at one remove, and gain perpetual pleasure at the paradoxical comparisons that continually arise from his two-faced mask of man of wit and woman; indeed the pleasure derives from the exact measuring of the distance of that remove—'Thus, *like* an arrant Woman, as I am'. This is a game that grows more difficult, but all the more worth playing, as the resemblances stretch and grow thin but still sustain through the inset personae of fine lady and true whore. The poem is composed of women betraying each other — and the other sex, too, insofar as it comes in their way—and is thus made up of a descending series of self-scrutinies, of measurements of the treachery that detachment from the human self entails, when a writer (for instance) stops living in order to sigh, in an impossible self-denying act of self-scrutiny, a remark like

> Were I (who to my cost already am
> One of those strange prodigious Creatures *Man.*)
> A Spirit free, to choose . . .

This construct made out of creative treacheries, this descending spiral of darker and darker illusion analysed, may explain Rochester's choice of a name for his heroine. The word 'Artemisia' means the species of bitter herb that contains the plant wormwood, and the poet may have thought this 'flower of Artemis' a good name for his sharp-tongued virginal heroine; but Rochester's impersonation of a female speaker suggests that he remembered the punchline of a story from Herodotus's account of the Persian Wars.[11] Artemisia, Queen of

[11] The relevant parts of Herodotus's *History*, Book VIII, chapters 87-8, here quoted in George Rawlinson's translation of 1858, had not been translated into English before Rochester's death, though there were both Latin and French

Halicarnassus, saved herself at the battle of Salamis by a brilliant act of treachery: hotly pursued by a Greek vessel and finding her way barred by one of her own allies, she promptly rammed and sank the allied ship. The Greek pursuer assumed that she must therefore after all be Athenian, and turned away; the observers of her own party assumed that the rammed vessel must after all be Athenian, and sang her praises. Xerxes said afterwards: 'My men have behaved like women, my women like men!'

In the circumstances this remark has complexities that resonate in the memory (though Herodotus did not think it his business to notice them); the likelihood is that they lingered in Rochester's, given the subtle and paradoxical games based on wars of the sexes that he goes in for in *Artemisia*, from the point of view of the unsexed, unsocial writer—

> Like Men that marry, or like Maids that woo,
> Because 'tis the very worst thing they can do.

For the poem traces a charming, casual course downwards from disloyalty to criminal treachery. The substance is so delightfully 'sociable', so randomly entertainingly gossipy, so thick with amusing observations of the known, that we barely notice its structure, which is hardly in fact extrusive: it may even be slightly flawed. But it has without doubt three descending stages. We open with the innocent but wilfully sentimental Artemisia's discovery of solaces for herself—from a social world that both governs and disgusts her—in the

---

versions. The story may have reached Rochester indirectly, but it is worth noting that most contemporary accounts support Parsons's description of the poet as 'thoroughly acquainted with all Classick authors, both Greek and Latin', and that Rochester seems to have had no less a taste for reading history than Lucius Cary, who a generation earlier was reading the Greek historians.

conscious follies and illusions of art, turning from a hated passionless love to a loved loneliness of letter writing. From there the poem moves by a refined malice on Artemisia's part to the inset treacheries of the 'fine lady', who is false not only to the other sex—her poor fool of a husband—but even to her own species, preferring the 'dirty, chatt'ring . . . Minature of Man', a monkey to be fondled instead of a human creature to be loved. And she herself glances down with a considering pity to the voiceless, unindividuated, merely type-treachery of Corinna, who—a kind of dark shadow behind the delicate Artemisia—also knows how to use her experience and others' for her own purposes, but who rests, 'diseas'd, decay'd', at the mortgaged bottom of society, 'looking gay', 'talking fine', her every feeling a lie and her whole life an illusion — her child a 'Bastard Heir' to existence itself, the shadow of a shadow of a shadow. The poem climbs down through one level of fashion and fantasy to another, and then another as through a 'snare'—

(*Bedlam* has many Mansions; have a care)

—which catches us and lands us on the brilliant last line:

But you are tir'd, and so am I.
                    Farewel.

In a letter to his friend Savile, Rochester wrote: 'The World, ever since I can remember, has been still so unsupportably the same'. It is on that 'tired' insight into some pure banality in social existence that the poem rests, as on a rock. And later he wrote to the same correspondent, casually: 'few Men here dissemble their being Rascals; and no Woman disowns being a Whore'.[12] *Artemisia* is a kind of undissembled dissembling, an

---

[12] *The Rochester-Savile Letters,* ed. J.H. Wilson (1941), pp. 40, 73.

owned disowning, because it is a social construct itself, and gives genuine pleasure thereby: it is a letter to a friend just like these often delightfully witty friendly letters Rochester wrote to Savile, or the usually charmingly kind and nonsensical notes he sent home to his wife. But at the same time it expresses the weary lucidity of Rochester's insight into the social self: it is a progressively more ruthless, more searching light turned towards the darkness that cannot be either 'dissembled' or 'disowned'. And it is on that darkness, the lack of anything beyond the self-cancelling illusions of the poem, that it rests: there is nothing else, and nothing is what it is. At the centre of *Artemisia* is the fine lady who defines the aesthetic which both poem and social world are content to share, with a line that clearly haunted Swift's imagination: 'The perfect joy of being well deceiv'd'. So long as the poem lasts the poet is content to stay within that 'perfect joy', to follow out to the end his own curiously elegant, undoubtedly entertaining construct of lies and illusions: one that is successful enough to make many of its readers ask (as does Rochester's best editor), 'Which of the poem's many characters represents the truth?'—when the only answer is, 'Fewer and fewer and less and less'.

This is something like the answer, at any rate, which Rochester gives in his most powerful poem, the *Satire against Mankind*, whose finality is its essential character, at whatever stage of the poet's career it happened to be written. It is here that a reader may see most clearly the achievement and the cost of Rochester's peculiar art of extremity, the intensity he gained by arriving at the point where something comes to an end:

> Then Old Age, and experience, hand in hand,
> Lead him to death, and make him understand,
> After a search so painful, and so long,
> That all his Life he has been in the wrong.

I mentioned earlier Rochester's use of capitals, and the faltering rhythm that breaks his strongest lines. The peculiar character and memorability of this climactic fourth line is the way that capital L 'Life' quietly dissolves into wavering distractedly weak negatives—Man is not, but 'has been', he is nowhere but 'in the wrong'. This 'satire' is no satire, but simply a poem, which we cannot understand unless we believe its medium, its verbal surface; and this poem, which seems to have so much public clarity, in fact works through a style like a misty secret labyrinth in which the person who reads well gets lost,

> climbs with pain,
> *Mountains* of Whimseys, heap'd in his own *Brain*:
> Stumbling from thought to thought, falls head-long
> down.
> Into doubts boundless Sea, where like to drown,
> Books bear him up awhile . . .

It is, again, unsurprising that the best part of the poem, its harsh, undeniably conclusive opening prelude, moves from paradox ('who to my cost already am') to net us throughout in a rhetoric whose most memorable effects are all explicit intricacies of verbal surface, like that later famous obsessive passage in which the poet winds his subject, Man, in a knot of monosyllables:

> wretched *Man*, is still in Arms for fear;
> For fear he armes, and is of Armes afraid,
> By fear, to fear, successively betray'd
> Base fear . . .

Perhaps only Rochester among English poets could have got

such power from the exploration of that purely negative form of imagination, fear.

It may be asked how a writer whom I have presented as so concerned with 'Nothing' could have made of his work a 'something' still appreciated after three hundred years—indeed, enjoyed and admired now as at no other time since that period of intense success during which the poet himself wrote. I want to finish by suggesting an answer to this question: and it will be one other than the supposal that nihilism as such is peculiarly the concern of the present. Rochester was not a philosophical nihilist, and there is no reason to suppose that, if he were, the modern reader would admire him for it. But the reasons are, I think, in some sense philosophical, so long as we are content to allow that the philosophical can include the highly paradoxical. For Rochester can, like any other poet, be more relevantly 'philosophical' when he is writing entirely playfully, with an appearance of casual randomness, than when he 'thinks' in prose. Rochester's arguments with Burnet, for instance, are well worth looking at: but at their most interesting they only include points that will be put far more forcibly and personally in the verse, even where we might least look for it.

Thus, a reader interested in Rochester's philosophical position could do worse than read the Epilogue he wrote for a friend's comedy, *Love in the Dark* (even the title is Rochesterian, suggestive of that 'mistaken magic' he calls love in 'The Imperfect Enjoyment'), where he mocks the success of a rival company given to effects of flying spectacle:

> Players turn Puppets now at your Desire,
> In their Mouth's Nonsense, in their Tails a Wire,
> They fly through Clouds of Clouts, and show'rs of Fire.

A kind of losing *Loadum* is their Game,
Where the worst Writer has the greatest Fame.

These two brilliant images are better than they ought to
be—than any casual satire can be expected to be. This is surely
because Rochester was himself a kind of equilibrist, an expert
in moving high over that vacuity he defines in 'Love and Life':
no past, no future, no present to call his own, beyond a
'miraculous' minute high over the crowd. All his verse is,
similarly, a 'losing *Loadum*', a card-game like a slow bicycle race
where the loser wins, because he does the difficult thing. The
French Symbolist dramatist Jarry wrote a blasphemous essay,
which is genuinely funny and innocent, called 'The Crucifixion
considered as an Uphill Bicycle Race', which gets us within the
area where Rochester needs to be considered; remembering
Eliot's remarks on the relative spirituality of certain kinds of
blasphemy.

Rochester's angry antipathy to the worldly world of success,
that world in which for long he was so anxious to succeed and in
which he so long succeeded in succeeding, even to the point at
which the perhaps comparably worldly Bishop Burnet remarked
with some satisfaction after the poet's death, 'All the town is
full of his great penitence'—this world-opposing side of his
character was clearly far more evident to the other and probably
more intelligent attendant on his death-bed, Robert Parsons,
his Puritan mother's private chaplain. It was Parsons who
brought to Rochester perhaps his only moment of true spiritual
vision, by reading to him Isaiah's prophecy of the Suffering
Servant, the Messiah who is a man of no importance at all; and
it is Parsons, similarly, who in the sermon he preached at
Rochester's funeral at once grasped the game of 'losing Loadum'
the poet had played morally all his life:

> He seem'd to affect something Singular and paradoxical
> in his Impieties, as well as in his Writings, above the reach
> and thought of other men. . . . Nay so confirm'd was he in
> Sin, that he liv'd, and oftentimes almost died, a Martyr for
> it.[13]

It was surely this upside-down spirituality, or reversed idealism, that made Johnson among other eighteenth-century writers think that *Upon Nothing* was Rochester's best poem, for it is the single one of all his works which in its startling depth and largeness comes close to that classic standard, even to that image of Nature which Johnson demanded of his poets; for *Upon Nothing* is of course both cosmology and history, a mischievous rendering down of all those Renaissance histories that start with the Creation and end with the present day. Johnson, who had remarked casually to Boswell that 'Politics are now nothing more than means of rising in the world', would have appreciated Rochester's demonstration that *sub specie aeternitatis* they are also a means of falling in it:

> The great Man's Gratitude to his best Friend,
> Kings Promises, Whores Vows, tow'rds thee they bend,
> Flow swiftly into thee, and in thee ever end.

The liturgical cadence here, as in the music of an ancient Latin hymn gone slightly wrong in the translation, gives *Upon Nothing* something of that real largeness often lacking in Rochester's insubstantial verse—a verse that finally seems to hate substance—and makes of this poem an object with the

---

[13] Robert Parsons, *A Sermon Preached at the Earl of Rochester's Funeral* (1680), p. 9.

extension of a Rubens ceiling reversed, or a Purcell chorale re-set for solo flute. Or, to make comparisons within the poet's own work, *Upon Nothing* is empowered, by its source in the paradoxical encomium, to bring into the forefront those elsewhere entirely latent Metaphysical elements in Rochester's imagination, such as he himself tended to dismiss with irritation as the 'extravagances' of 'my fantastic mind'; elements which make, for instance, *A Ramble in St James's Park*, when it is compared with the reductive and mean-minded work of Butler which it so admiringly seems to copy, an actual if finalizing perpetuation (for all its grossness) of earlier Renaissance modes of idealism, rather than a Butlerian destruction of them.

It is in this high and spacious abstraction that *Upon Nothing* contrasts so interestingly with another 'nothing' poem, the very late translation from Seneca's *Troades*. The best lines of this translation are those in which the poet picks up and adds to the essential materialism of his source:

> Dead, we become the Lumber of the World;
> And to that Mass of Matter shall be swept,
> Where things destroy'd, with things unborn are kept...

Bodies here become disturbingly indestructible, like old dressmakers' dummies stacked among the dusty attics of Chaos: the Lumber image has a humorous irritated homeliness in considering physical existence that is the other side of the coin to Rochester's idealism. Clearly, it was the very closeness and actuality of the Restoration poet's sense of the physical and material world—the inevitabilities of his 'realism', the close limits of the only vision he knew, like the small confines of the court he was ironically drawn to—that threw him back on an idealism markedly negative, abstract: such as Rochester himself found in another Roman poet, Lucretius, after whom he splendidly invoked gods who needed nothing, asked nothing, were angered by nothing. And similarly he maintained against Burnet's Christian God—a god deeply marked by that recurring pragmatism that can make English theology, as Coleridge once remarked, as insistently vulgar as it is realistic—that

> God had none of those Affections of Love or Hatred, which breed perturbation in us, and by consequence he could not see that there was to be either reward or punishment. He thought our Conceptions of God were so low, that we had better not think much of him: And to love God seemed to him a presumptuous thing, and the heat of fanciful men.[14]

It is easier to see, or rather to feel, the flaws in the theology of the time if we turn the kind of over-pragmatism that the romanticism in Rochester was struggling with into its more secular philosophical form: the Hobbesian philosophy that entered deeply into the imagination of the age, even into areas where nothing was consciously felt but angry hostility to Hobbes's premises. Hobbes's philosophy has more power than Burnet's theology simply because it relies more deeply on and speaks more frankly from its age's historical presuppositions than any true theology can honestly do. It is possibly easier to write a *Leviathan* out of mid-seventeenth-century history—out of the disillusioned consciousness of the age—than to create a work of dogmatic theology out of it. Hence the potency of a passage that says:

> The whole mass of all things that are, is corporeal, that is to say, body . . . also every part of body, is likewise body, and

---

[14] Gilbert Burnet, *Some Passages of the Life and Death of John, Earl of Rochester* (1680), pp. 52-3, quoted in Farley-Hills, *Critical Heritage,* p. 60.

hath the like dimensions; and consequently every part of the universe, is body, and that which is not body, is no part of the universe: and because the universe is all, that which is no part of it, is *nothing*; and consequently *nowhere* . . .[15]

Where the religious imagination of a period becomes hopelessly comfortable, a conformist cul-de-sac, more life *may* be found latent in the world of blasphemy or heresy. Thus, even the intensely 'social' Henry James—whom I cite, as having used him elsewhere in this essay—at the end of the nineteenth century turned, like many good writers after him, to the murky world of the ghost story, to express moral and spiritual facts not easy to keep hold of otherwise within the philistine insensibility of contemporary middle-class England. The real subject of *The Turn of the Screw*, as he made clear in a letter, was the appalling exposure of children to lethal adult affections; it was to help him out in saying this, to a society of hard sentimentalists, that he called up the pot-boiling spooks, for whom he apologizes to his correspondent, jokily: 'I evoked the worst I could . . . "Excusez du peu!"'[16] Rochester, two centuries earlier, had 'evoked the worst *he* could': he evoked half-lovingly that 'Nothing' which Hobbes laid down like a Green Belt at the edge of his unimaginably material universe, whose 'body', in the light of what Rochester does with *his* 'Nothing', takes on something of that ghostly immateriality which the poet gave mockingly to *his* 'bodies'—the lovers who haunt his poems.

Such negativism deserves, I think, the highest respect: it should not be brushed aside, in anxious search for more substantial virtues—more positive philosophical values. Rochester's Nothing deserves, what is more, even more respect in that it entails for the poet something of a losing game, a

[15] Hobbes, *Leviathan*, *ed. cit.*, p. 440.
[16] Lubbock, *Letters of Henry James*, I, 308.

'losing Loadum'. To refuse, in all honesty, to trust the only world one has; to find oneself incapable, on the other hand, of any other music in one's poetry beyond the crash of breaking glass—this is a fate as grim as that appalling epitaph with which Johnson sums up the fate of Harley: 'Not knowing what to do, he did nothing; and, with the fate of a double dealer, at last he lost his power, but kept his enemies'. Rochester clearly possessed that extreme moral courage that is willing to leave behind a body of work fundamentally 'unlikeable'—that presents the self in it as unlikeable, for the work's sake: a moral courage which is the prime virtue, one would have thought, of all true artists. For, from inside Rochester's work, which is likely to have come from a personality both sensitive and generous as well as honest, no 'nice man' emerges. There is only an image strikingly like that image, now in the National Portrait Gallery, which we mainly know Rochester by: a portrait surely planned and dictated to the painter by the poet himself, and so an actual picture to match those several verse 'Instructions to a Painter' which were a favourite literary exercise in this period. Half turned away from his audience, whom he regards with a sideways and wary inward amusement, the Earl of Rochester welcomes us with an open gesture of his shining silk left arm, which gesture at the same time directs our eyes to his raised right hand holding a laurel wreath high over the head of a pet monkey; a monkey who, like an image in a mirror, gives to the poet with his left hand a torn fragment from the book he grips open with his right. In aesthetic terms, the animal is the focus of the human being, while reversing his every gesture: its little black mask is raised devoutly towards the white unforthcoming stare that the tall young aristocrat directs down on us; the monkey's small chest slightly unnerving in its nakedness against the costly concealing taffetas that fall from a lace collar over the man's torso. Like his own 'fine lady', the poet is playing with a 'Minature of Man'.

In itself the portrait is a design of pure rebuttal, all dead ends and barriers. It is an impassive self-concealing refusal of disguise, a courtier's serious joke about looking 'frightfully': it takes us back, that is to say, to the elder Wilmot's remark, and summarizes what I have tried to say about an art of social surface. For all such charm as the Rochester portrait has is not a charm of 'personality', but is a matter of the subtle shadowings of the taffeta cascading down below the intelligent but rebuffing eyes of the poet, the silk's beauty sharpened by contrast with the disturbing nakedness of the small ape's chest beneath its blank dark averted mug. Underneath the taffeta there is to all intents and purposes nothing whatever: but the picture is not, for all that, empty—it is full of something, even if that something is couched in mockeries and denials.

Rochester and the Metaphysicals

JOHN WILDERS

In his essay on 'The Social Background of Metaphysical Poetry'[1] L.C. Knights makes a sharp qualitative distinction between the achievement of the poets of the early seventeenth century, in particular Donne and Herbert, and those of the Restoration, Dryden and Rochester. The work of the former is, he points out, characterized by a recognition of 'the multiple nature of man', an ability to communicate the belief that to be human is to live 'simultaneously at many levels', the spiritual, the sensuous and the intellectual. 'In the best of Donne's love poems', he explains, 'there is active not only passion or affection but a ranging and enquiring mind and a spirit capable of perceiving values.' And, conversely, 'the most ecstatic experience is felt in terms "which sense may reach and apprehend".'

The essential difference between the Metaphysical poets and those of the Restoration is, according to Knights, that the latter failed to do justice to the complexity of their own—and human —nature. Whereas formerly, as he puts it, 'man had been recognised as a complex being, rooted in instinct, swayed by

[1] L.C. Knights, 'The Social Background of Metaphysical Poetry', in *Further Explorations* (1965), pp. 99-120.

passion, and at the same time an intellectual and spiritual being, he is now something much simpler', 'a reasonable creature in the limited way in which the new age understood "Reason" '. The literature of the Restoration, he concludes, 'tends to stress the rational and social elements in man to the exclusion of other qualities'. The cause of this decline, this narrowing of the range of poetry, are to be found, Knights believes, in the changes in the cultural life of the court and the aristocracy between the Jacobean age and that of Charles II, and the shift from a medieval conception of man as a complex organism to a Hobbist, empiricist view of man as a more simply physical, mechanical being.

It is not my intention here to question Knights's judgement of the Metaphysicals. On the contrary, I am sure he defines very precisely some of the qualities for which they are to be admired. Nor shall I enquire into the social and philosophical changes which took place during the middle of the seventeenth century. These have been frequently and amply treated elsewhere. My more limited concerns are to try and rescue one Restoration poet, Rochester, from the charges of narrowness and simplicity, to show that from his best poems, as from Donne's, we acquire what Knights calls 'a renewed sense of the multiple nature of man', and to argue that, although Rochester's tone of voice—his grace, lucidity and harmoniousness—is that of a court poet of the Restoration, his mind is as much aware of its complexity as were those of his predecessors. The contradictoriness of Rochester the man is apparent to anyone at all acquainted with his life. Contradictoriness is also, I believe, the distinguishing mark of his work.

In one of his frequent moments of self-analysis, Donne perceived that he was 'a little world' composed both of physical 'elements' and 'an Angelike spright'. His most characteristic poetry is a record either of the tensions between these

conflicting and incompatible parts of which he is made, or of
those moments of extreme feeling when they seem miraculously
to have become reconciled. The struggles between the physical
'elements' and the 'Angelike spright', between the needs of the
body and the aspirations of the soul, are recorded most
intimately in his religious poems where, as he says, 'to vex me,
contraryes meete in one', and where he repeatedly prays that,
through his own faith and the grace of God, he may subdue the
flesh and find stability in a submission to the divine will:

> O Holy Ghost, whose temple I
> Am, but of mudde walls, and condensed dust,
>   And being sacrilegiously
> Halfe wasted with youths fires, of pride and lust,
>   Must with new storms be weatherbeat;
>   Double in my heart thy flame,
> Which let devout sad teares intend; and let
> (Though this glasse lanthorne, flesh, do suffer maime)
> Fire, Sacrifice, Priest, Altar be the same.

Seldom in his *Divine Poems,* however, does Donne claim to
have achieved that resolution of the discordant elements within
himself for which he begs. Nor, probably, could he expect to do
so, for to be human was, by definition, to be in a state of civil
war. He is, like all men, a self-contradicting, paradoxical
creature, at the same time temporal and eternal, substantial yet
insubstantial, a thing of earth yet destined for heaven and
living, meanwhile, like a stranger in an alien land. Hence he
repeatedly defines his sense of his own dividedness through the
use of paradox, for what is death to the body is life to the soul;
those are his 'best days' when he 'shakes with fear', and the Lord
throws down in order that he may raise.

The *Songs and Sonets*, too, with their intricate argument-
ation and tortured rhythms, create an impression of struggle
even when their ostensible purpose is to record moments of
harmony and equilibrium. Mutually shared, fulfilled love is
often triumphantly celebrated as an experience which, though
physical, can by its sheer intensity and violence transmute the
participants into a state of transcendence in which they are no
longer the prisoners of space and time but are capable of
encompassing all places and becoming impervious to change:

> She is all States, and all Princes, I,
>   Nothing else is.
> Princes doe but play us; compar'd to this,
> All honor's mimique; All wealth alchimie.
>   Thou sunne art halfe as happy as wee,
>   In that the world's contracted thus . . .

Yet we sense that these and Donne's other bold assertions of
the power of love to raise him above his fleshly limitations are
not as unreservedly self-assured as they appear to be.

This impression is created, I believe, by his use of metaphor.
Unlike simile, metaphor affirms the total and absolute identity
of subject and predicate, the lack of distinction between the
thing described and the means used to describe it. To assert
that 'she *is* all States and all Princes I' is not the same as to
suggest that, in their relationship, he is to her as a prince is to a
state or that, in certain limited respects, they resemble all states
and princes. To use a metaphor is to make a statement which is
at the same time true and untrue, true figuratively but untrue
literally. We should, obviously, look in vain for the name of
Donne's mistress in a map of the world, yet in another sense,
accepted as true only because of the conviction with which it is
expressed, she is, indeed, all states and he all princes. By using

metaphor rather than simile Donne makes us aware of the doubts of which he is himself conscious even—indeed, especially—when he is at his most emphatic. He does, needless to say, use similes, but his most powerful and subtle statements are made in the form of metaphors:

> yet all these seeme to laugh,
> Compar'd with mee, who *am* their Epitaph.

> Oft a flood
> Have wee two wept, and so
> Drownd the whole world, us two; oft did we grow
> To *be* two Chaosses, when we did show
> Care to ought else; and often absences
> Withdrew our soules, and *made us* carcasses.

Such statements are at the same time true and false and testify to Donne's awareness of his own uncertainty even when he claims to be most certain. They are a form of paradox.

In other poems he creates the impression of simultaneously believing and disbelieving his assertions by expressing an obviously simplified point of view which does not represent the whole, complex truth as he himself is capable of seeing it. Hence at one moment, in 'The Anniversarie', he can rejoice in the enduring constancy of his love, and at another, in 'The Indifferent', he can pride himself on his limitless talent for inconstancy; he can, in 'The Exstasie', argue that the union of bodies is the physical expression of the union of souls, and in 'Loves Alchymie' revile love as a 'vaine Bubles shadow'. Both kinds of poem are expressions of half truths. To be in love is for Donne, as for Shakespeare, at the same time to experience 'the nobleness of life' and to make 'the beast with two backs'. By assuming an extreme, simplified attitude, he allows himself to voice opinions which are recognized as only partially true. The complexity of his nature is implied by the inadequacy of his expression of a mere part of it.

The most appropriate form in which such dichotomies can be expressed is, obviously, the dialogue, and many of Donne's poems read like one side of a dialogue, an appeal to a God who is too remote to respond, or the refutation of an argument we have not been allowed to hear. The poet who found his most natural form in the dialogue, however, was Marvell, who in the pastoral dialogue between Clorinda and Damon and the dialogues between the Resolved Soul and Created Pleasure and between the Soul and Body voiced the struggles between the opposing sides of his own nature. The 'Dialogue between the Soul and Body' consists of a series of statements and counter-statements, each one of which is made up of paradoxes, so that not only are the Soul's complaints challenged by those of the Body, but the paradoxical assertions made by each of them are self-refuting, as in the Soul's outcry,

> What Magick could me thus confine
> Within anothers Grief to pine?
> Where whatsoever it complain,
> I feel, that cannot feel, the pain.
> And all my Care its self employes,
> That to preserve, which me destroys:
> Constrain'd not only to indure
> Diseases, but, whats worse, the Cure:
> And ready oft the Port to gain,
> Am Shipwrackt into Health again.

Marvell lucidly and succinctly defines the painful, absurd paradox of being human. Very properly he does not try to bring his argument to a conclusion. To resolve the conflict in the poem would be to oversimplify his own nature. It therefore stops abruptly; it does not conclude.

It was possible, as the poets of the seventeenth century discovered, to create a dialogue out of an existing poem by writing an answer to it, and a minor tradition, that of the answer poem, evolved in this period, of which a typical example is Suckling's lyric, 'Hast thou seen the Down in the air', an answer to Ben Jonson's 'Have you seen but a bright Lillie grow'. Whereas the last line of Jonson's Petrarchan poem is 'O so white! O so soft! O so sweet, so sweet is she', Suckling's answer concludes, 'Oh so fickle, oh so vain, oh so false, so false is she!'. Suckling's lyric is a parody of Jonson's, and although parody is often no more than a display of mimicry it can also be a form of counter-statement, a rebuttal in which the style but not the point of view of the original work is reproduced. The various parodies in *As You Like It* serve this function. Orlando's verses in praise of Rosalind are an expression of idealized, platonic love, and Touchstone's reply to them is more than a display of ingenuity:

> If the cat will after kind,
> So be sure will Rosalind.
> Winter garments must be lin'd,
> So must slender Rosalind.

Touchstone's parody is composed on the assumption that love is no more than a 'lust of the blood', and, indeed, throughout *As You Like It* Orlando believes that love is a yearning of the spirit and Touchstone sees it as a desire of the flesh. Each character perceives a half truth, and the audience, observing all the characters, is made aware of what Knights calls 'the multiple nature of man'.

A similar dramatic technique is used by Suckling in his

dialogue 'Upon my Lady Carliles walking in Hampton-Court Garden', in which 'T.C.' (or Thomas Carew) responds idealistically to the prospect of Lady Carlisle, and 'J.S.' (or Suckling himself) takes the opposite, 'common sense' point of view. 'Didst thou not find the place inspir'd?' asks the platonist Carew,

> And flow'rs as if they had desir'd
> No other Sun, start from their beds,
> And for a sight steal out their heads?
> Heardst thou not musick when she talk't?
> And didst not find that as she walkt
> She threw rare perfumes all about
> Such as bean-blossoms newly out,
> Or chafed spices give?

To which the empiricist Suckling confesses,

> those perfumes (*Tom*)
> I did not smell; nor found that from
> Her passing by, ought sprung up new,
> The flow'rs had all their birth from you
>
> .   .   .   .   .   .
>
> Alas! *Tom*, I am flesh and blood
> And was consulting how I could
> In spite of masks and hoods descry
> The parts denied unto the eye;
> I was undoing all she wore,
> And had she walkt but one turn more,
> *Eve* in her first state had not been
> More naked, or more plainly seen.

Suckling's dialogue brings us practically into the world of

Restoration comedy, the world of Etherege and Rochester.
Although the language of this pleasant literary exercise has
none of the strength and particularity of Marvell, it does
indicate that the latter was not the only poet writing in the
middle of the seventeenth century to be aware of the
contradictions between the imaginings of the spirit and the
impressions received by the senses. Nor did this preoccupation
simply cease on the accession of Charles II. Dryden examined it
philosophically in *Religio Laici*, Butler treated it satirically in
Hudibras,[2] and it was given a new, unique expression by
Rochester.

If David Vieth's chronological arrangement of the poems is
correct, then two of Rochester's earliest works were written in
the form of dialogues,[3] and very shortly afterwards he and his
wife composed a pair of love lyrics in the form of a protestation
and an answer, both of which are to some extent paradoxical in
sentiment.[4] Rochester's own lyric opens with a resolution to
reprimand his wife for being false to him and to retaliate by
being unfaithful to her. His self-confidence soon fails him,
however, and he confesses that he cannot help but be true to
her and begs her to be kinder to him, since without her love he
must expire:

> Give me leave to rail at you
> (I ask nothing but my due):
> To call you false, and then to say
> You shall not keep my heart a day.

---

[2] Samuel Butler, *Hudibras*, ed. John Wilders (1967), Part II, Canto ii, lines 77-84.
[3] 'A Pastoral Dialogue between Alexis and Strephon' and 'A Dialogue between
Strephon and Daphne', *The Complete Poems of John Wilmot, Earl of Rochester,*
ed. David M. Vieth (1968), pp. 4-9.
[4] I am grateful to Dr Raman Selden of the University of Durham for pointing out
to me the relevance of these two poems to this discussion.

> But, alas! against my will
> I must be your captive still.
> Ah! Be kinder, then, for I
> Cannot change, and would not die.

There is little in this first stanza to distinguish it from a score of courtly, cavalier love poems. As the lyric concludes, however, the 'kindness' for which he begs is made to appear less conventional:

> It gilds the lover's servile chain
> And makes the slave grow pleased and vain.

Lady Rochester, it now appears, is being asked to act in collusion with her husband in order to induce in him a state of satisfying but despicable self-deception.

This concluding argument seems to undermine the very cause it is ostensibly being used to support, and love itself is shown to be at the same time a fulfilment and a subjection of the personality of the lover. The paradoxes, however, do not end here, for in her 'answer' to her husband's plea, Lady Rochester argues that the 'kindness' for which he begs is not the way to secure his affections and that, though she loves no other man, she must feign contempt for him in order to keep him true to her:

> Though you still possess my heart,
>   Scorn and rigour I must feign;
> There remains no other art
>   Your love, fond fugitive, to gain.

Moreover each poem, fairly complex in itself, hints at further complexities in the other. If we return to Rochester's contribution to the dialogue once more, we may now wonder whether the ultimate motive behind his plea for gentleness is the need not for servitude but for that promiscuity which, according to his wife, it encourages. Though superficially artless, the two poems hint at the simultaneous and irreconcilable desires for fidelity and infidelity expressed elsewhere in Rochester's lyrics and at the contradictions of his motivation. It is impossible to know whether the husband's plea is designed to deceive his wife or himself or neither of them, or (to put it another way) whether either of the poems is consciously or unconsciously ironical, or not ironical at all.

In certain respects Rochester's lyric 'Against Constancy' is written in the tradition I have tried to sketch out. It is a witty defence of sexual promiscuity in the manner of Donne's 'The Indifferent', or of the 'Defence of Women's Inconstancy' in the *Paradoxes and Problemes*. Here again, like Donne, the poet strikes a deliberately challenging posture; he assumes the simplified role of the libertine. This is also, as Jeremy Treglown has pointed out,[5] an answer poem, a reply to or rebuttal of such declarations of faithful, idealized love as Henry King's 'Tell me no more how fair she is' whose opening line it echoes. The two lyrics, King's and Rochester's, can be read as companion pieces, opposing arguments in a debate which, in combination, put forward first the Platonic and then the empirical views of love. What is new is partly the aristocratic condescension of Rochester's tone, the seemingly confident assumption that sexual fidelity is the last refuge only of the stupid and the impotent, and the effortless assurance that he and his fellow libertines are distinguished from the 'duller fools' by virtue of their sexual potency and versatility:

[5] Jeremy Treglown, 'The Satirical Inversion of Some English Sources in Rochester's Poetry', *Review of English Studies,* NS 24 (1973), 43-4.

But we, whose hearts do justly swell
   With no vainglorious pride,
Who know how we in love excel,
   Long to be often tried.

There is in his 'longing to be often tried' a daring to take on
the risks which lesser men shun, a readiness to be repeatedly
challenged like a warrior eager for combat. But the language of
the final stanza casts doubt on the kind of heroism which is
being flaunted. For one thing, Rochester descends for the first
and only time to specific, practical details—

Then bring my bath, and strew my bed

—and the domesticity of these details makes his exploits appear
mundane. Moreover the language (and consequently the tone)
of the last stanza is not nearly as cool as that of the rest of the
poem. It is taken from a different register:

Then bring my bath, and strew my bed,
   As each kind night returns;
I'll change a mistress till I'm dead —
   And fate change me to worms.

Far from seeming free to experience limitless variety, he now
appears trapped in an obsession, frantically performing a
mechanical act designed to challenge the inescapable nullity of
death. As the poem ends, we are made to wonder who are the
more self-deceived, the 'cold men and fools' who have no
alternative but to be constant, or the poet whose notion of
'advancing higher' is repeatedly to engage in tests of his sexual
potency until the flesh to which he has dedicated himself
decomposes. The poem renders unacceptable the very course

of action it purports to recommend. It is paradoxical, and if we re-read it in the light of its final stanza, we are induced to wonder whether its opening lines are ironical or not:

> Tell me no more of constancy,
>   The frivolous pretence
> Of cold age, narrow jealousy,
>   Disease, and want of sense.

Is Rochester attempting to convince the reader or does he want to seem to be trying to convince himself? Like Donne, Rochester can create the impression of an underlying insecurity at the very points when he seems most assured. Far from being the statement of a simple point of view, the poem reveals a divided mind unable wholly to embrace the kind of life it seems to defend.

The complex effects created by this poem arise from the disjunction between the controlled, easy harmoniousness of its rhythms and the violence of its language, a feature also of Marvell's work, and it is extraordinary that such subtleties can be achieved in a language which is consistently plain, precise and lucid—language which one would expect to be incapable of subtlety. A similarly limpid diction and effortlessly fluent rhythm reappears in 'A Song of a Young Lady to Her Ancient Lover', the metre of which is similar to that of Jonson's 'To Celia':

> Come my Celia, let us prove
> While we may the sports of love.

But although Rochester's Song is also Jonsonian in the purity and neatness of its diction, the impression it makes on the reader is a great deal more disturbing:

Ancient person, for whom I
All the flattering youth defy,
Long be it ere thou grow old,
Aching, shaking, crazy, cold;
   But still continue as thou art,
   Ancient person of my heart.

On thy withered lips and dry,
Which like barren furrows lie,
Brooding kisses I will pour
Shall thy youthful [heat] restore
(Such kind showers in autumn fall,
And a second spring recall);
   Nor from thee will ever part,
   Ancient person of my heart.

There is no need to emphasize that Rochester is here assuming a role, one of his characteristic procedures, and how far he expects us to sympathize with the young lady's sentiments it is impossible to decide. The troubling effect created by the poem again arises from a disjunction between its sentiments and its language. The tone of the lady's declaration of constancy, created by the easy, regular rhythms, is tender and affectionate, but her attentions are bestowed on an object which is made repellent, and the most powerful language describes the effects of age and decay. The feelings—of altruism, fidelity and loving care—are conventionally admirable. Do they cease to be admirable when lavished on an 'ancient person'? The poem expresses the combination of attraction and revulsion which Rochester consistently felt towards sex. It does justice to his sense of his own divided nature.

The poem 'Absent from thee, I languish still' is, as Anne

Righter (now Anne Barton) has said, 'the best of Rochester's lyrics',[6] indeed one of the great love poems in the language. It is distinguished by its extraordinary honesty. The poet knows that only in the love of the woman he is addressing (possibly his wife) can he find lasting peace, and yet he also knows that he must inevitably be unfaithful to her. This is, again, an expression of a divided mind, a self-contradicting personality which longs to be faithful to the only object worthy of his devotion and yet realizes in the moment of pledging that fidelity that he must betray her. To be honest is not the same as to be simple:

> Absent from thee, I languish still;
>   Then ask me not, when I return?
> The straying fool 'twill plainly kill
>   To wish all day, all night to mourn.
>
> Dear! from thine arms then let me fly,
>   That my fantastic mind may prove
> The torments it deserves to try
>   That tears my fixed heart from my love.

Even though he knows in advance that the infidelities of which he will be guilty must be 'torments', he is compelled by his self-destructive nature to pursue them. It is remarkable that a state of mind as complex as this is described with the greatest economy, simplicity and lack of strain.

The lyricism of Rochester's love poems—the effortless flow of the rhythms, the occasional gentle stress on the significant word, the lingering harmoniousness of the rhymes—shows his indebtedness to Ben Jonson and the cavalier poets. But

---

[6] Anne Righter, 'John Wilmot, Earl of Rochester', *Proceedings of the British Academy,* 53 (1967), 67.

Rochester is very much more than what Knights says he is, 'the most gifted of the mob of gentlemen who wrote with ease', and the feeling expressed is not, as Knights believes, 'simple, a momentary tenderness'. The combination of lyrical tone and tortured sense produces an effect quite different from that of Suckling or Herrick. Rochester's is the voice of a man grown so familiar with his own self-destructiveness that it causes him no surprise. The very unstrained quality of his style makes his honesty the more chilling. I am sure Knights is right to recognize in him the influence of Hobbes and seventeenth-century empiricism; after all, Hobbes is actually quoted in the poems.[7] That, holding as he did a view of human nature much simpler than that of Donne and Herbert, he was still able to do justice to his own 'multiplicity', makes his achievement the more impressive.

---

[7] The second stanza of 'Love and Life' (Vieth, *The Complete Poems*, p. 90) is derived from *Leviathan,* as Treglown points out.

The Professional Amateur

PETER PORTER

Rochester's reputation as a poet is hedged by confusions, presumptions and downright prejudices. It is not possible to write about his poetry with that detachment which would be expected in the case of any other poet as eminent and as long dead. Of the two main reactions, uneasiness with his poetry's sexual content has proved less debilitating than modern huffiness at his being one of the nobility. Perhaps this attitude is not so modern, since it lies behind Pope's dismissive remark that Rochester was 'a holiday poet'. Yet Rochester is not only the most accomplished English poet between Milton and Pope, but prefigures, in his own heroic couplets, that tone of deep-cutting urbanity which is Pope's mark of style, and which becomes the most effective instrument of invention in English poetry after the Caroline high noon.

There are important things Rochester could do which were alien to Pope (writing lyrics which are so much more than song-texts for instance), and even more important ones which Pope was master of and which lay outside Rochester's ability. The point is not that Rochester is Pope's equal or Dryden's superior, but that he passed on the baton to Pope and thereby to the rest of English poetry. It never went through Dryden's hands.

Many of one's own prejudices must be declared, if not cleared away, before the verse itself can be decently assessed. Rochester's male chauvinism (countered by his willingness to invest women with the highest independence as swashbucklers), his diabolism, his clubbableness, his aristocratic disdain for publishing, his insistence on drinking and telling, his death-bed conversion—all these are qualities which make him an uneasy figure for literary people to handle. We clerkly persons have never been much at ease with the Restoration writers, especially the court Wits. This distance was already apparent to Pope, no leveller but a man of the affluent middle class who did not care for self-destruction and diabolism. But Rochester, like all the best writers, shows us the restless human spirit moving in a universe where morality only becomes itself after it has been tested by experience. He and his friends were much more than cynical show-offs. They were the sons and heirs of long-exiled cavaliers, men and women distrustful even of their own legitimation. Behind their masks of fashion, their charades to relieve boredom and their sexual predatoriness, was a Hobbesian anxiety about the state itself. What would hold up, what would keep anarchy at bay? Certainly their privileges meant much to them, but they had few illusions about them. What came back with King Charles was anxiety as well as idleness and horseplay. We should consider the hangover Cromwell's protectorate must have given the following generation. Under him serious music flourished, the state enjoyed deep peace and there was little sequestration of property or interference with the opponents of the Commonwealth. There can never have been so liberal a dictator as Cromwell, and the expansion of England, to become both an imperial power and a moral force in the world, was begun by him.

Many of King Charles's courtiers saw this well enough, though they would have wished some other source of it. The Restoration led to a diminution of England's seriousness and effectiveness. There was nothing to do but act up. Rochester demonstrates, in the brief passage of time between his teenage poems welcoming the King's return and the sombre late masterpieces, a whole spectrum of disillusion with his friend the King, and with the whole of what we would now call the English Establishment. The motives behind his most scurrilous satires and lampoons were certainly not all disinterested or moral ones, but there is an undoubted element of frustrated patriotism among them. Rochester was always a man to go too far, and there is an impossibilist, idealist side to his scorn:

> All monarchs I hate, and the thrones they sit on,
> From the hector of France to the cully of Britain.

With this frustrated patriotism goes Rochester's classicism. He translated a number of Latin passages which suggest his philosophical viewpoint, that of the disciplined pagans such as Lucretius and Seneca. The way the Roman poets wove their theology into a realistic picture of life as men must endure it appealed to Rochester—at least, if we go by what he chose to render from their works into English. His version of lines 44 to 49 of *De Rerum Natura* may be no more than a brief exercise, though the fragment could simply be all that survives (together with a more tentative version of the opening of the poem) of a larger undertaking. But even in isolation, these lines form a beautifully apt statement as fine as anything ever put into epigram form:

> The gods, by right of nature, must possess
> An everlasting age of perfect peace;
> Far off removed from us and our affairs;
> Neither approached by dangers, or by cares;
> Rich in themselves, to whom we cannot add;
> Not pleased by good deeds, nor provoked by bad.

It is doubtful that Rochester could have kept this up, but I am tempted to show how precise and poetical his mind was by contrasting his version with that of the same passage by an admired poet of our own day, C.H. Sisson:

> Divine nature cannot be other than nature
> Subsisting for endless time in an unspoilt peace
> Far away from ourselves and the things that touch us;
> For deprived of pain, and also deprived of danger,
> Able to do what it wants, it does not need us.
> Nor understands our deserts, and it cannot be angry.

Rochester's direct involvement with the classics is tiny beside the translations of them made by Dryden, or Pope's use of them as perennial touchstones, exemplified in *An Essay on Criticism.* But his frame of mind recalls one Latin poet particularly, Martial. It has usually been understood, if not often acknowledged, that poetical skill is not the same thing as 'poetical temperament'. Neither Martial nor Rochester had such a temperament. They were realists first, exaggerators afterwards, and transcendentalists almost never. Later on in this article I shall liken Rochester's work to that of modern American writers, to Wallace Stevens and John Ashbery. But I don't mean to suggest that he had any trace of Emersonian sublime in him. He became almost an analyst of language because of his impassioned detachment, yet his temperament was classical. Martial looked at Domitian's and Trajan's Rome in very much the way Rochester regarded Charles's England: appalled by fools more than he was upset by knaves. Classicism means keeping technique in the foreground. It suggests that hatred of humbug is a better guiding principle than righteous indignation. Rochester and Martial join hands across the centuries in being castigated as the dirtiest poets in the pantheon. They should not mind the opprobrium, if they can also claim credit as the greatest realists.

There is ample evidence in Rochester's work of a pleasing gentlemanly lightness and detachment. There is also, as everyone knows, some coarseness of sensibility; but nowhere will one find carelessness. Amateur, in the old and correct sense, Rochester was, since he did not challenge the convention of the time which kept gentlemen from publishing. But he was not amateur at versification, and his freedom from the restraints of the market, together with his restless imagination, led him to become an innovator, the chief mark of his innovation being a lightness in the use of the couplet which was his direct gift to Pope. His dozens of squibs and lampoons also show a rhythmic and syntactical freedom which is quite unlike carelessness. Even the broader pieces in ballad rhythm aim for epigrammatic memorability rather than the anacreontic longwindedness produced by the more knock-about Restoration versifiers:

> To some cellar in Sodom Your Grace must retire
> Where porters with black-pots sit round a coal-fire;
> There open your case, and Your Grace cannot fail
> Of a dozen of pricks for a dozen of ale.

When one considers pieces like this, a whole armoury of light-verse lampoons with their air of improvisation, one is at the heart of the suspicion with which literary critics have tended to look at Rochester. Many famous (and professional) poets wrote similar pieces, if less well; but their scatological works are customarily set apart from their main output, and are seen as deliberate relief from high-mindedness. Rochester's case is different: his main compositions and even his more deliberately decorous writings are likely to break into scatology at any moment. It is this gentlemanly looseness which criticism has been uncomfortable with. Rochester's unwillingness to separate large formal designs from the improvising of a rhymers' club has done his reputation harm.

The case is even stronger if his songs and lyrics are considered. In their splendid ease of utterance, in their perfect judgement of what is transferable to verse from the lineaments of music, and in their memorability, they are the finest lyrics between Shakespeare and W.H. Auden. They are essentially etchings in lyricism, townee vignettes, if set against the wash-and-watercolour of the great English lyrical tradition—Keats and Tennyson, for instance. Yet while these song pieces can be exquisitely limned and as far as possible from all raucous effects, they can also be libidinous and anti-Romantic. Generations of commentators have relished the lyric called 'Love and Life', especially its first stanza:

> All my past life is mine no more;
>   The flying hours are gone,
> Like transitory dreams given o'er
> Whose images are kept in store
>   By memory alone.

but it is no more perfect or delicate in tone than 'A Song of a Young Lady to Her Ancient Lover', 'The Mistress', 'To a Lady in a Letter' and 'On Mrs Willis'. I might seem to be stretching things in claiming delicacy for these last two sets of quatrains, but I find the term just when the almost lacy precision of Rochester's writing is examined:

> Whom that I may describe throughout,
>   Assist me, bawdy powers;
> I'll write upon a double clout,
>   And dip my pen in flowers.

Here, as so often, Rochester is realistic and original, and his amused recognition of the disrupting effect of the uneuphemistic language of the upper class on the make-believe of poetry contributes largely to his modernity. It is, after all, something to be the only writer with a claim to classical standing in English literature who directly refers to menstruation. And to this taste for realism he adds imaginative conceits which raise some of his pornographic poems to the level of fantasy. It is not certain whether Rochester wrote *Sodom*, but there is reason for thinking it was composed by a group of wits including him. In one scene there is a splendid example of tenderness dressing up as obscenity for its own protection, which, if it is his, expands one's appreciation of his use of pornography in poetry. The scene where Prince Prickett and Princess Swivea enact a kind of sexual catechism is very funny and at the same time sweet. Here is some part of that elusive Arcadian sexuality we have heard about from populist libertarians. When the Princess shows him her cunt, she explains:

> It is the workhouse of the world's great trade;
> On this soft anvil all mankind was made.

I cannot imagine a more reflective and gentle description. Even the jokey realism of their encounter is without any desire to hurt:

> *Prickett*: I'm in. I vow it is as soft as wool.
> *Swivea*: Then thrust and move it up and down, you fool.

But pornography is morally equivocal, to say the least. *A Ramble in St James's Park* is excellent poetry by any standards, but it doesn't hesitate to 'do the dirt on sex' (in D.H. Lawrence's priggish phrase). Style intervenes, of course, as it does more tastefully in the gamier songs. The whole poem is more comic exaggeration than disgust. It is Rochester's way to impose ruthlessness on ranting, so that verbal baroque becomes well-pictured grotesquerie:

> But cowards shall forget to rant,
> Schoolboys to frig, old whores to paint;
> The Jesuits' fraternity
> Shall leave the use of buggery;
> Crab-louse, inspired with grace divine,
> From earthly clod to heaven shall climb;
> Physicians shall believe in Jesus,
> And disobedience cease to please us,
> Ere I desist with all my power
> To plague this woman and undo her.

With such imaginative conceits, Rochester inflates his black comedy to high artifice. Pope carried this way of writing to its apogee in *The Rape of the Lock* ('Maids turned bottles cry aloud for corks'), and in some of his Horace imitations (themselves owing much to Rochester's *An Allusion to Horace*). He might have found the crab-louse's progress apt, but his good taste would have precluded his using it. Nor would he have been happy with the casual reference to religion which follows. Even more Popean is the fantastical pastoral sketch of the Park which occurs early in the poem:

> There, by a most incestuous birth,
> Strange woods spring from the teeming earth;
> For they relate how heretofore,
> When ancient Pict began to whore,
> Deluded of his assignation
> (Jilting, it seems, was then in fashion),

Poor pensive lover, in this place
Would frig upon his mother's face;
Whence rows of mandrakes tall did rise
Whose lewd tops fucked the very skies.
Each imitative branch doth twine
In some loved fold of Aretine,
And nightly now beneath their shade
Are buggeries, rapes, and incests made.

Put into pentameter, this could be a fantasia on Piero di Cosimo carried out by a less cautious Alexander Pope.

'Signior Dildo' exhibits the same exaggeration, but this time ventures into the ballad form and the anacreontic. It is hard to know whether libertine raillery such as Rochester's is merely male chauvinism, or whether it has a serious undertone. Rochester may be scolding what Vieth calls 'the promiscuous noblewomen of the Restoration Court' because their flagrant affairs could lead to instability of privilege and the state. If that notion seems pitched too high, it might be more reasonable to suggest that 'Signior Dildo' at least among his lampoons is unflinching in locating sexual lust as the prime effrontery offered by aristocratic women:

The Countess of Falmouth, of whom people tell
Her footmen wear shirts of a guinea an ell,
Might save the expense if she did but know
How lusty a swinger is Signior Dildo.

Rochester's development as a poet was steadily towards greater exuberance. His earliest poems, such as 'A Dialogue between Strephon and Daphne', already assault the pastoral eclogue with the shock tactics of irony and surprise endings but they stick pretty closely to the mode they mock at. Only a few years further on, though a long way to advance in so short a life, we find him in 'The Mistress' perfecting a genre of realistic love poem which is truthful, ambiguous and yet passionate. There are slight echoes of the Strephon and Daphne exchange in this poem, but its tone is quite different. Cleverness and cynicism have fled, and so have mechanical contrivances. Irony, an awareness of mixed feelings, has taken their place. The poem abounds in received phrases and examples from poetic stock, but they are never used without being specially placed in an ever-expanding field of irony. I think it worthwhile to quote the poem entire. It is quite long by the standards of Rochester's lyrics, but no stanza is dispensable if it is to be fully understood. The antepenultimate stanza, for instance, one of the finest declensions in his entire corpus, must come exactly where it does in the argument.

> An age in her embraces passed
>   Would seem a winter's day,
> Where life and light with envious haste
>   Are torn and snatched away.
>
> But oh, how slowly minutes roll
>   When absent from her eyes,
> That feed my love, which is my soul:
>   It languishes and dies.
>
> For then no more a soul, but shade,
>   It mournfully does move
> And haunts my breast, by absence made
>   The living tomb of love.
>
> You wiser men, despise me not
>   Whose lovesick fancy raves
> On shades of souls, and heaven knows what:
>   Short ages live in graves.

Whene'er those wounding eyes, so full
    Of sweetness, you did see,
Had you not been profoundly dull,
    You had gone mad like me.

Nor censure us, you who perceive
    My best beloved and me
Sigh and lament, complain and grieve:
    You think we disagree.

Alas! 'tis sacred jealousy,
    Love raised to an extreme:
The only proof 'twixt her and me
    We love, and do not dream.

Fantastic fancies fondly move
    And in frail joys believe,
Taking false pleasure for true love;
    But pain can ne'er deceive.

Kind jealous doubts, tormenting fears,
    And anxious cares, when past,
Prove our hearts' treasure fixed and dear,
    And make us blest at last.

In the 'Dialogue between Strephon and Daphne', the end is a cynical shock, the girl explaining, with a touch of O. Henry, that she has been unfaithful all along while her more sententious lover was working himself up to his disclosure of intent. It reads like an exercise. 'The Mistress' is well stocked with paradox, it begins seriously and spaciously, in a near Petrarchan manner, but the irony is planted from the start:

these quatrains, as has often been pointed out, sound almost ecclesiastic, Isaac Watts *avant la lettre.* Rochester keeps up the Neoplatonic tone, but he mixes proverbial drinkers' wisdom with it. It is a song, after all, and you can feel a presence such as Campion's behind it—solemnity and levity enjoying the same stately metre. The fourth stanza is very Campion-like—'Short ages live in graves'. Cynicism is shown as the proper path to truth. There are no shocks, no *trompe-l'oeil*, and there is nothing indecent. Instead, we have a profound view of love offered by a sceptic whose experience of fashion and pleasure has given him a taste for extremes.

In this sense Rochester is a forerunner of Baudelaire and Rimbaud. His 'déréglement du sens' was more thorough than theirs because it was not programmatic. The blessing at the end of the poem is the knowledge (very bitter knowledge) that the greatest felicity on earth depends upon a fixed antipathy of natures, that true love feeds on anxiety and betrayal. None of this is new to literature: what is purely Rochester's is the mixture of tones he uses to accomplish his vision. In the end the drinking songs, the lampoons, the extemporisations and variations on classical obscenity helped Rochester crown his lifetime's serious work — a description of the schizophrenic nature of love and of society.

About a dozen lyrics, another dozen lampoons and half a dozen satires may make a small arsenal with which to raid immortality, but Rochester's proportion of successes to failures is very high, and he died almost as young as Shelley. In all his finest works there is a distinctive mixture of realism and restlessness, and especially an exasperation with the human condition, where godlike traits and vile impostures live side by side. Most poets feel this way, especially if they have any bent for satire, but Rochester seems to have been set off by an impatience with himself and with the art of poetry. He was

Dorimant, but he was a lot more besides: he seems not to have been able to charm the misanthropist in himself. His satire is therefore wide-ranging and beyond faction. Sometimes he can be genial and occasionally he snarls, but generally his tone is made up of despair that human imagination takes people so quickly into pretence and folly, as though he is glossing Hamlet's ambivalent praise of the creature Man to Rosencrantz and Guildenstern.

His poetry offers one of the best opportunities known to me to study the chronic ambivalence of seriousness in a creative imagination. People being so little capable of reform, the satirist's railing must defend itself against the charge of self-indulgence. It often does this by going too far. Rochester will almost redeem mankind by making it heroically preposterous. But then his realism intervenes. His poetry, whether in the social form of the couplet, or in lyrics, strives towards a formal satisfaction which its author's restless imagination will not permit to prevail. His finest works snatch defeat from the jaws of victory, and do it in the name of truth.

Rochester's special quality as a poet is his pursuit of Nothing, his supreme adaptation of *sprezzatura* to a point where it anticipates the twentieth-century artist's concern for the purpose and value of poetry itself. This questioning of a calling in the calling's own highest attainment is at its most developed in his long poems, especially *Artemisia to Chloe, A Satyr against Reason and Mankind* and *An Allusion to Horace. Upon Nothing* itself, though a fine poem, is a mechanical development of well-worn philosophical tropes. *Artemisia to Chloe* shows morality as a house of mirrors, but its censure is very ambiguously placed. On the one hand, there is the famous encomium of love, seemingly (if its context weren't so equivocal) as serious as any written by a professional eulogist:

That cordial drop heaven in our cup has thrown
To make the nauseous draught of life go down;
On which one only blessing, God might raise
In lands of atheists, subsidies of praise . . .

In this manner, Fiordiligi and Dorabella croon in Act One of
Così fan tutte, as they bid farewell to their lovers going to the
wars — 'Soave sia il vento'. They are true, they are serious: it is
the world which doesn't fit such sentiments. Later in
Rochester's poem, experience suggests a more cynical form of
husbandry, a variation on Daphne's response to Strephon—
'Womankind more joy discovers / Making fools, than keeping
lovers.' Fool-making is seen as woman's preferred business. It
may be the only form of revenge readily available to women:

A woman's ne'er so ruined but she can
Be still revenged on her undoer, man . . .

But the cynicism is etched in lightly. Rochester seems to
suggest that the world must go on, that its occupation is just to
be itself. He would have sympathized with the smoothly
sententious arguments of the auctioneer Sellem in Stravinsky's
and Auden's *The Rake's Progress*: 'Truly there is a divine
balance in Nature: a thousand lose that a thousand may gain.'
Sellem calls the scavengers at his auction 'Nature's mission-
aries'. Under all the scars of its realism and its misanthropy,
Rochester's satire still adopts the missionary position. After all,
it has a clearer target than human folly—its belief in itself, the
value inherent in writing poems well. The paradox is that the
man who questions the very existence of art, or at least its
usefulness, must, if his case will be heard, be a supreme
practitioner of it. Setting out to discover what poetry is for, and
what it can do, is a way of writing it, a legitimate source of

inspiration. Rochester, the gentleman who must be seen to eschew professionalism (the one waylaid in *Timon,* who disclaims that he is the author of some verses which are the admiration of the town—'A song to Phyllis I perhaps might make, / But never rhymed but for my pintle's sake'), becomes in practice the disinterested poet, the writer not above prejudice but free from faction.

It is possible to trace in all Rochester's finest work a virtuosity of disengagement—from the cordial drop, love, from fidelity, from the social order, from moderation and good sense, and especially from the claims of poetry itself. It is perhaps unwise to draw parallels between artists in ages widely separated from each other, but I detect in Rochester that taste for examination of language, for pursuing poetry into its own words, which is the mark of much verse written this century, especially that of Wallace Stevens and John Ashbery. By concentrating upon the impossibilism of poetry's high calling, Rochester achieves an art which will not serve, which is without utility, but which has more presence than that of its rivals.

The simplest way to demonstrate this is to put any Rochester passage up against one by Dryden or even by Pope. Rochester's verse has a quite different feeling: it is heavier and lighter at once; it upbraids without wishing to reform; it ignores good taste but is always elegant; it even eschews too much regularity of diction or prosody yet is rhythmically precise, fastidious as sound. It is the true voice of human despair lamenting that however great our attainments we must fall ludicrously below the gods. In the end it has no absolute to offer beyond its own existence. Stevens and Ashbery, as aesthetes, are self-conscious atheists. Rochester's atheism is equally profound. His goes beyond the Americans', and extends to a total distrust of reason and philosophy which they are too respectful of the academy to dare allow.

Filling with frantic crowds of thinking fools
Those reverend bedlams, colleges and schools;

. . . .

And we have modern cloistered coxcombs who
Retire to think, 'cause they have nought to do.

In the three hundred years since his death, Rochester has slowly come into his own. We hear that he was almost too celebrated in the 1670s, when his most audacious pieces were circulating in the town. 'One man reads Milton, forty Rochester', reports *Poems on Affairs of State.* Perhaps Milton might have enjoyed him, as Marvell did — Vieth records that the indecent song, 'Have you not in a chimney seen' is attributed to Milton in *Oxford and Cambridge Miscellany Poems, 1708.* Rochester has always had devoted supporters, and just as vehement deprecators. He has never been entirely forgotten, so perhaps it matters less that today he is likely to be praised for the wrong reasons. He is not some wild outsider clamouring for clever people like ourselves to hear his voice: instead, he is a brilliant classical poet cheated of full recognition by a combination of literary laziness and critical priggishness. In his lifetime he made the gesture of snubbing respectable fame, and the revenge taken has been a long one. Once encountered, however, his poetical presence is irresistible. However much or little he is studied, he is lovingly and repeatedly read.

What came after Rochester has done nothing to lessen the freshness and verve of his writing. And his appeal will always in part be his misanthropic exaggeration. Few poets as devoted to realism as Rochester have been so in love with form: even fewer masters of the high style of English verse have been willing to accommodate not just the vulgar but the life-denying. Rochester smuggles more unpoetic matter into great poetry than any other English master. Perhaps he was a true professional after all.

'He knew my style, he swore'

JEREMY TREGLOWN

Considering how distinctive a tone of voice Rochester's is
generally thought to be, it's surprising how many other people's
voices have been mistaken for it. David Vieth's edition, based
on the fullest study so far of the state of the texts, prints
seventy-five poems, and seven additional ones there is doubt
about: in all, less than a third of the corpus attributed to
Rochester in Restoration and eighteenth-century collections—
the undependable collections on which his literary reputation
was partly founded, and the undependable corpus accepted
more or less wholesale by editors and biographers, including
some in the twentieth century: John Hayward, Johannes Prinz,
Ronald Duncan, Graham Greene.

Of course, there were many reasons for wanting to foist
poems on him—not least that his name was good for sales. Of
the falsely or mistakenly attributed poems, however, many are
not only very good, but good in ways that have been thought
peculiarly characteristic of 'the mad Earl'; it must have been
easy three hundred years ago, as it still is today, to be genuinely
mistaken. Rochester's poems are, for example, well known to
be often irreverent, obscene and extremely funny. But so,
sometimes, are those of his friends and acquaintances Aphra
Behn, Buckhurst (Earl of Dorset), Etherege, Oldham, Sedley
and the others who between them wrote almost half of the
contents of the first printed collection attributed to him, the

1680 *Poems on Several Occasions by the Right Honourable the E. of R.* And most of these authors wrote in one or other of the literary conventions for which Rochester is famous. Erotic pastoral, poems with a new angle on the subject of sexual 'enjoyment', classically-modelled literary and social satire, were all fashionable modes.

Faced with these facts, and with additional complications like the joint authorship of many Restoration poems, it's tempting to concentrate on what the court poets have in common, and indeed a scholarly critical text of their works would be useful, not least because it would bypass some of the irrelevancies of the attribution debates. All the same, it is an interesting fact that an increasing awareness since the 1940s— particularly fostered by John Harold Wilson and David M. Vieth—of Rochester's membership of a group, and of the artistic claims of some of the group's other members, has coincided with a heightening of his own reputation, and a growing sense of his individuality.

One of his qualities, I want to suggest, is an idiosyncratic complexity of tone which, though it can be found in some individual poems by his contemporaries, is uniquely pervasive in his own work: so much so that it unifies the otherwise disparate lyrics and satires that can confidently be attributed to him, as well as the poems of both kinds written in dramatic voices. *Timon,* Rochester's satirical narrative about a dinner party, is a good place to begin, since the poem itself starts with a false attribution. Timon describes to a friend how the previous night he was waylaid by an importunate acquaintance who dragged him off to dinner, praising him on the way for his authorship of a poem he didn't write:

> He takes me in his coach, and as we go,
> Pulls out a libel of a sheet or two,

Insipid as the praise of pious queens
Or Shadwell's unassisted former scenes,
Which he admired, and praised at every line;
At last it was so sharp it must be mine.
I vowed I was no more a wit than he:
Unpractised and unblessed in poetry.

. . . .

He knew my style, he swore, and 'twas in vain
Thus to deny the issue of my brain.
Choked with his flattery, I no answer make,
But silent, leave him to his dear mistake,
Which he by this had spread o'er the whole town,
And me with an officious lie undone.

It's an effective way in to the story, establishing as it does a reason for what we will find is a special interest of Timon's: good judgement, whether in literature, food and drink, conversation or manners generally. This is the subject of the poem, though it is not an 'essay' in the sense of Pope's more deliberated *Moral Essays*; and by a *bouleversement* characteristic of Rochester the satire is itself, arguably, in poor taste: a vivid, contemptuous account of a dinner party at which Timon is, however unwillingly, a guest, reviling the appearance, behaviour and conversation of his hosts and fellow guests behind their backs and criticizing the quality of the meal.

This kind of coexistence of positive and destructive attitudes in Rochester's work has often been noticed. What is so effective in *Timon* is the deftness with which they are worked together. It is seen in an indirect way in Timon's account of the literary talk at the meal, when Halfwit praises Orrery's play *The Black Prince:*

> His sense so little forced that by one line
> You may the other easily divine:
> 'And which is worse, if any worse can be,
> He never said one word of it to me.'
> *There's* fine poetry! You'd swear 'twere prose,
> So little on the sense the rhymes impose.

The joke is not simply the praise of the prosiness of Restoration heroic poetry (did Arnold know the poem, one wonders?) On the one hand, Rochester's own couplets provide a sharp, flexible example of what writing in couplets can be, and on the other the quotation itself (in the play, 'And which is worse, if worse than this can be, / She for it ne're excus'd her self to me') has been distorted so as to exaggerate its faults. Repeatedly throughout the party, the guests are made to seize on and praise passages which are obviously bad. When Kickum, for example, rhapsodizes on Crowne's line 'Whilst sporting waves smiled on the rising sun', Timon observes 'Waves smiling on the sun? I'm sure *that's* new'; the same disingenuous gambit he used with his acquaintance at the beginning of the poem, 'I vowed I was no more a wit than he'.

The superficial blandness of irony like this typifies Rochester at his most dangerous: dangerous not only in the internal fictions of his poetry, but to the unguarded reader. I have written elsewhere about the court poets' ironic use of quotation and allusion,[1] but a couple of hitherto unrecorded examples in the work of Rochester—who does it more than anyone else— may be excused at this point. The first is the likelihood, pointed out to me by Howard Erskine-Hill, that the fragment 'Sab: Lost' beginning 'She yields, she yields', is a reversal of Milton's

---

[1] Especially in 'Scepticism and Parody in the Restoration', *Modern Language Review*, 75 (1980), 18-47.

Comus, where Sabrina won by freeing the lady from the enchanted chair in which the lecherous Comus trapped her. (The poem stands in relation to the earlier work like 'Grecian Kindness' to *The Trojan Women*.) The second, which I owe to Kenneth Palmer, occurs when Rochester alludes to Marvell by way of satirizing the sexual morals of Charles II. The poem beginning 'I'th' isle of Britain, long since famous grown' describes the King in a famous couplet: 'Restless he rolls about from whore to whore, / A merry monarch, scandalous and poor'. It seems possible that there is a side-glance here at Marvell's heaven-reflecting drop of dew, an emblem of the soul:

> Restless it rolls and unsecure,
>   Trembling lest it grow impure,
> Till the warm sun pity its pain,
> And to the skies exhale it back again.

These are moments — there are scores of them in the poems — when Rochester depends on the reader to recognize a literary reference in order to catch his tone, to feel the full weight of his otherwise unobtrusive irony. This is an elusive kind of art, and to be alert to what he is doing, it is helpful to know his views on tone. For a writer so resistant to theory and so unsystematic in his thinking he is remarkably clear on the subject. There is, as has often been pointed out, his Augustan support of reason and common sense. But this takes a particular form in his scorn for the effortful. Timon's tiresome acquaintance is satirized at the beginning of the poem above all for his persistence — the relentlessness with which he urges Timon to come to dinner ('The longer I denied, the more he pressed') and the doggedness of his praise of the verses he assumes Timon wrote, 'Which he admired, and praised at every line'. Similarly, the hostess is mocked for her effortful charm, in a line whose extra stress mimes the effort—'Shē with her ŏld blĕar eȳes to smīte begūn'; the host for the energy of his ministrations (the beef is so heavy that it makes the servant carrying it sweat; the bottle 'briskly flies about'); and everyone is ridiculed for the vigour of the talk as much as for its lack of discrimination: the poem ends with their falling to blows and Timon's departure, vowing 'nevermore / To . . . hear the hectors roar'.

This is snobbery of manners of a kind familiar in Restoration comedy. Rochester does it even better in a conversation in *Tunbridge Wells* which anticipates Pope's minute attention to social vacancy:

> Here waiting for gallant, young damsel stood,
> Leaning on cane, and muffled up in hood.
> The would-be wit, whose business was to woo,
> With hat removed and solemn scrape of shoe
> Advanceth bowing, then genteelly shrugs,
> And ruffled foretop into order tugs,
> And thus accosts her: 'Madam, methinks the weather
> Is grown much more serene since you came hither.
> You influence the heavens; but should the sun
> Withdraw himself to see his rays outdone
> By your bright eyes, they would supply the morn,
> And make a day before the day be born.'
> With mouth screwed up, conceited winking eyes,
> And breasts thrust forward, 'Lord, sir!' she replies,
> 'It is your goodness, and not my deserts,
> Which makes you show this learning, wit, and parts.'
> He, puzzled, bites his nail, both to display
> The sparkling ring, and think what next to say,
> And thus breaks forth afresh: 'Madam, egad!
> Your luck at cards last night was very bad . . .'

and so on.

As the gallant's laborious metaphor about the sun and the damsel's eyes reminds us, social and literary manners are usually interchangeable, though they were more so in this period than in most. Rochester finds practically any kind of effort ludicrous: metaphysical effort, in the mountain-climbing passage near the beginning of *A Satyr against Reason and Mankind*; political effort, too, in a letter to Savile comparing politicians to boys struggling to get crab apples.[2] But he is particularly scornful of effortful writing: the attempt to amuse, 'Which blundering Settle never could attain, / And puzzling Otway labours at in vain', or the endeavours for which Dryden is lampooned in the same poem, *An Allusion to Horace*: 'Five hundred verses every morning writ / Proves you no more a poet than a wit'. The most damaging way he could begin an attack on Scroope was to satirize him as needing 'To rack and torture thy unmeaning brain / In satyr's praise'. Elizabethan and Jacobean writers had satirized literary bombast and preciousness; Dryden was to attack dull writing; Pope, among other things, pedantry. Rochester is the first English writer to have concentrated his attack on people who tried too hard. There may be no reason to assume he wrote with particular ease, but he would have taken Pope's line about the mob of gentlemen as a compliment.

If in Rochester's fluent verse an appearance of effortlessness provides a self-validating and, in the contrast with what he parodies, very funny criterion of poetic taste, its concomitant chilliness can seem less attractive when he is writing about sex. In one of his more patronizing letters to his wife, he criticizes her for being 'high spirited', by which he probably meant standing up to him:

---

[2] *The Letters of John Wilmot Earl of Rochester,* ed. J. Treglown (1980), p. 119.

[I] cannot deny to you that Heroick resolutions in woemen are things of the which I have never bin transported with greate admiration nor can bee if my life lay on't for I thinke it is a very impertinent virtue . . . tollerable only in a waiting gentlewoman.[3]

Several of his lyrics begin with a similar mixture of the jocular and the suavely cool, leaving the speaker's mood to be nervously guessed at, and this is particularly the case when he is criticizing effortful behaviour: 'Insulting beauty, you misspend / Those frowns upon your slave'; 'What cruel pains Corinna takes / To force that harmless frown'; 'Phyllis, be gentler I advise'. 'The Imperfect Enjoyment', of course, is all about the consequences of trying too hard, or at least wanting too keenly—'Eager desires confound my first attempt'. And in one of his best, most elusive poems, the speaker begins by encouraging her partner to reduce his efforts—

> I could love thee till I die,
> Wouldst thou love me modestly,
> And ne'er press, whilst I live,
> For more than willingly I would give.

Taken out of context, this emphasis on Rochester's suavity might be in danger of suggesting an effete kind of poet, as supinely aloof as the Lucretian gods by whom he was indeed attracted. But of course this is only one side of his contradictory poetic personality, and it coexists in an idiosyncratic way with another, quite different: the garrulous, the fantastical, the sometimes ferociously engaged. Timon's narrative, whatever his posture of detachment, is one unstoppable flood of detailed

[3] ibid., pp. 75-6.

anecdote, from the moment, six lines into the poem, when he replies to his friend, to his abrupt conclusion 171 lines later. The sheer continuity of the story, with its sequacious, copious realization of the scene, establishes a narrator only partially given over to irony. His joke about his hostess's talkativeness ('She had run on, I think, till now') rebounds on Timon in a way lightly reinforced by his forgetful (so to speak) self-identification at some points with the guests he otherwise mocks. 'Left to ourselves', he says in the first person plural, 'of several things we prate'; the line can be read as acknowledging the incompleteness of his isolation.

This might not seem a generalizable argument. It could be objected, for example, that there isn't any comparable contradiction of the detached narrative stance in the similarly contemptuous *Tunbridge Wells.* Yet the exaggeration of the speaker's misanthropy in that poem, the intensity of the revulsion with which the 'squeamish' narrator 'silently slunk' from one part of the town to another before choosing, like Gulliver in 'A Voyage to the Houyhnhnms', the nobler company of a horse, if not ironic, is hard to take uncritically. And once again the implied claim of superiority is belied by the involvement evident in the poem's close observation—for example in the passage about the gallant just quoted.

What *Tunbridge Wells* also obviously shares with *Timon* is its straightforward treatment of events in the order in which they occur, without any major organizational scheme except chronology and with only the most perfunctory of beginnings and endings. *Timon* is started off by a questioner who then disappears, and the poem ends very abruptly. *Tunbridge Wells* begins abruptly and ends with a simple moral reflection. This linearity is typical of Rochester's satires, with the exception of *Artemisia to Chloe.* Even in *A Satyr* he seems to have made up the argument as he went along, partly in response (as

David Trotter shows) to current attitudes and events.[4] And the contrast with *Artemisia*, with all that poem's distancing devices of voice within voice and story within story, only emphasizes how the other satires belie the poet's aloofness by seeming to spring impulsively from his lips. This impression may have been the result of deeply contemplated effort, but it's very convincing—so much so that Johnson said Rochester's poems were mostly such as one fit of resolution might produce. He is the first poet in English to write satires—as distinct from lyrics (Donne and his imitators taught him a lot)—which, however artful their metre and rhymes, sound like someone talking. The satires of Wyatt and Donne are too convoluted to succeed in this, despite the vituperativeness of their indignation: their morality is too fully preconceived to allow Rochester's air of hectic improvisation. And of Restoration satirists Marvell, Oldham and Dryden all, if in different ways, seem much more fully in charge of what they are saying.

This is often called self-assurance: 'Augustan confidence'. But in so far as confidence is at stake, the poems of these contemporaries of Rochester are surely as much the result of the opposite: of the knowledge that every effective lampoon would be responded to and attacked, and so needed to be as nearly watertight as the author could make it. Rochester rarely concerns himself with anticipating criticism or stopping gaps in his argument: the most he does in *A Satyr against Reason and Mankind* is to counter possible exceptions to his case with a qualification in the closing couplet. He was famous for making up verses impromptu—'Rhyme to Lisbon', the impromptus on Charles II and Louis XIV, the two extempores about clergymen. There is every likelihood that 'Signior Dildo', too, for example, was composed rapidly in company: its basis—rhyming on all

[4] See below, pp. 111-32.

the gossip-worthy names he could think of or had suggested to
him—is like that of a party game.

Fertile extemporization characterizes the more boisterous
passages in his most obscene poems, 'The Imperfect Enjoyment'
and *A Ramble in St James's Park*—particularly the curses, with
their almost self-generating couplets:

> May your depravèd appetite,
> That could in whiffling fools delight,
> Beget such frenzies in your mind
> You may go mad for the north wind,
> And fixing all your hopes upon't
> To have him bluster in your cunt,
> Turn up your longing arse t' th' air
> And perish in a wild despair!

or

> Worse part of me, and henceforth hated most,
> Through all the town a common fucking post,
> On whom each whore relieves her tingling cunt
> As hogs on gates do rub themselves and grunt,
> Mayst thou to ravenous chancres be a prey,
> Or in consuming weepings waste away;
> May strangury and stone thy days attend;
> May'st thou ne'er piss, who didst refuse to spend
> When all my joys did on false thee depend.

The passages are a good example of the usefulness, in gauging
Rochester's tone, of remembering his views on effort; and of
the importance, in reading him, of common sense. Some critics
have detected sexual anxiety in passages like these, but that
'depend' seems a peculiarly subtle, wry pun for an anxious man

to be making. One of the things that are so enjoyable about these poems, with their Ovidian comic fury, is the fantastical detail with which the frustrations they describe are given their imaginative potency. Rochester is no more 'psychically impotent', in Dustin H. Griffin's phrase[5] (whatever it means) than is Kingsley Amis. 'The Imperfect Enjoyment' and *Jake's Thing* both liberate sexual anxieties because the situation they describe is clearly temporary — a fact suggested by the very alienation which the circumstances produce between the subject and his object. What Rochester wishes on his own Thing in his concluding curse is venereal disease: not a complaint to which the chronically impotent are very vulnerable. Once again in his poetry, but in a peculiarly physical way, detachment and engagement are made to coexist.

'The Imperfect Enjoyment' belongs to a minor genre of seventeenth-century lyrics on the same subject and is related to yet others which give a clue to Rochester's attitudes and help to explain his tone. These are 'lucky minute' poems. The theory of the lucky minute (or the 'happy minute' or the 'shepherd's hour') was that anyone who offered himself sexually during it would succeed. The idea is expounded in a poem by John Glanvill called 'The Shepherd's Hour', dated 1686, in which the 'happy Time' or 'lucky Minute' is described as the moment when 'a just Daring proves no Crime, / And feeble Pride resists in vain'.[6] Dorimant alludes to it in *The Man of Mode*:

> *Dorimant*: 'Music so softens and disarms the mind . . .'
> *Harriet*: '. . . That not one arrow does resistance find'
> *Dorimant*: Let us make use of the lucky Minute then.[7]

[5] Dustin H. Griffin, *Satires Against Man: The Poems of Rochester* (1973), p. 121.
[6] John Glanvill, *Poems: Consisting of Originals and Translations* (1725), p. 113.
[7] Act V, Scene 2.

Dryden, too, was familiar with it:

> Fair *Iris* and her Swain
>   Were in the shady Bow'r;
> Where *Thyrsis* long in vain
>   Had sought the Shepherd's hour.[8]

Seeking the hour was the catch, of course: there was no predicting the lucky minute. Glanvill complains:

> Ah Fate! to Man what Favour dost thou show,
>   Thus one kind Minute to bestow,
>   Yet let him not that one foreknow!

But this disadvantage was balanced by the fact that when the minute came, it allowed no social distinctions. It is this egalitarianism that marks the triumphant conclusion of Rochester's 'As Chloris full of harmless thought':

> Thus she, who princes had denied
>   With all their pompous train,
> Was in the lucky minute tried
>   And yielded to the swain.

Dryden offers a comic inversion of the lucky minute in his song 'Calm was the Even, and cleer was the Skie',[9] part of a neglected contemporary tradition similar to that of 'The Imperfect Enjoyment'. It may be described as the Lost Opportunity. Dryden's version presents a woman's account of her efforts to seduce Amyntas, who is hopelessly incapable of

---

[8] *The Poems of John Dryden,* ed. J. Kinsley (1958), p. 561.
[9] ibid., p. 126.

exploiting his lucky minute. His response is a nervous laugh: 'when with a fear he began to draw near, / He was dash'd with A ha ha ha ha!' Ironically, Amyntas thinks of himself as conventionally bold: 'you are cruel', he tells the salacious Sylvia, 'to keep your poor lover in awe'. But when at last he is persuaded to live up to his ideal of himself, he has missed his chance. The couple are interrupted by the arrival of another shepherd:

> as he grew bolder and bolder,
> A Shepherd came by us and saw;
> And just as our bliss we began with a kiss,
> He laughd out with A ha ha ha ha.

There are many contemporary variations. One, a parody of Dryden's poem by an unknown author, begins 'Sharp was the Air, and cold was the Ground' and attributes the lover's failure to old age, cold weather, smoke from a fire and coughing.[10] Another is Etherege's 'See how fair Corinna lies',[11] in which the speaker reproaches a 'dull' shepherd for not exploiting his opportunity with Corinna, and urges him to press his advantage 'While the happy minute is'. Yet another is provided by Buckhurst. In 'At noon, in a sunshiny day'[12] Chloris sits 'knotting' in the shade, apparently observed by no one except the narrator, whose responses are contrasted with the innocence of what she is doing, of the pastoral setting and of Chloris herself, who is described as 'innocent and gay':

> Each slender finger play'd its part,
> With such activity and art,

[10] In *Mock Songs and Joking Poems* (1675), p. 129.
[11] *The Poems of Sir George Etherege,* ed. J. Thorpe (1963), p. 31.
[12] *The Works of the English Poets from Chaucer to Cowper,* ed. A. Chalmers (1810), VIII, 343.

As would inflame a youthful heart,
And warm the most decay'd.

Chloris's suitor, 'bashful' Strephon, arrives and she abandons her knotting to give him 'such a call, / As would have rais'd the dead' (the *double entendre* is obvious). She invites Strephon to rest in her lap, an invitation which he interprets literally and accepts, promptly falling asleep. Chloris leaps up and attacks his dullness in a speech whose contemptuous references to his flocks and dismissive 'Go, milk thy goats' suggest that this inhabitant of Arcadia knows there is a world elsewhere.

If opportunism is a motif in individual poems by his contemporaries, though, it is a key to all of Rochester's verse, connecting his sexual attitudes with his headlong narratives, arguments and impromptus. And it is opportunism which gives his tenderest lyrics their undertow, a mixture of irony with something warmer: part humour, part good humour, and in both cases purposefulness. There are few lyrics of his, however elegiac, apologetic or reflective their ostensible mood, which don't suggest getting into bed: either the speaker and the spoken-to getting into bed together, or the spoken-to getting into bed with other people so that the speaker is left free, or the spoken-to letting the speaker get into bed with other people, or some other permutation. Indeed, it is his calmest poems, the ones where the language is closest to that of religious poetry, in which these ideas often turn out to be most actively pressing. 'Absent from thee I languish still' is a poem which asks the woman to let the speaker go away and then let him return 'To thy safe bosom' where he will 'expire', 'contented'. The sexual implication is obvious, though the whole poem is more complicated than the drawing out of this single aspect allows one to suggest; it is that if she won't have him back sexually, as well as in other ways, he will go away again: 'May I contented there expire', he says, 'Lest, once more wandering . . .'. Similarly, 'Love and Life' is at least partly designed to distract the woman's attention from what he has been doing in the past and will do in the future ('talk not of inconstancy, / False hearts, and broken vows') in order to bring her round to his ideas for the present moment.

Both these poems are partly saying what is said in the Chorus of the song 'Injurious charmer of my vanquished heart', which—like the others—depends on a familiar interweaving of spiritual and sexual ideas which amounts to an extended kind of *double entendre*, brought into the open in the last word:

> Then let our flaming hearts be joined
>   While in that sacred fire;
> Ere thou prove false, or I unkind,
>   Together both expire.

Just as the contemptuous, detached tone of *Timon* and *Tunbridge Wells* is held in balance with a more positive kind of imaginative engagement, so these verses, whose measured, unhappy facing of facts has brought them plenty of attention, have a compensatory wit—in all senses of the word—which can make mere 'seriousness' look narrow-minded. Their movement of tone, a kind of reconciliation occurring through the very progression in time of the words as we read them, is found in his letters, too:

> 'Tis not an easy thing to bee intirely happy, But to bee kind is very easy and that is the greatest measure [part] of happiness; I say nott this to putt you in mind of being kind to mee, you have practis'd that soe long that I have a joyfull confidence you will never forgett itt, but to show

that I myself have a sence of what the methods of my Life seeme soe utterly to contradict, I must not bee too wise about my owne follyes, or els this Letter had bin a booke dedicated to you & publish'd to the world, itt will bee more pertinent to tell you that very shortly the King goes to Newmarkett & then I shall waite on you att Adderbury. . .[13]

Of course, this characteristic tone of voice, with its interplay of engagement and detachment, physicality and spirituality, activity and reflection, can't be used to solve problems of authorship. Others have written divided poems, and in the absence of external evidence 'Injurious charmer of my vanquished heart' must stay where Vieth puts it, among the dubia. All the same, Rochester's is a style which can be characterized from the body of poems we are sure are his, and three hundred years on it has not lost its ability to intrigue, amuse and move its readers.

[13] Treglown, *Rochester's Letters,* p. 228.

Affairs of State

BASIL GREENSLADE

'Affairs of state', in the many collections entitled *Poems on Affairs of State* of 1689-1704, and in the Yale series derived from them, extend in practice to most aspects of the public life of the seventeenth-century political nation: king, court, Parliament, the Church, the town, the theatre, and a literary world over part of which presided the 'suburban Muse'.[1] My subject is narrower in scope—Rochester and what the period understood by 'business', or government and politics. In the conditions of the time the distinction is inevitably arbitrary, but for present purposes it is I think intelligible and serviceable. In reality, as Henry James put it, 'really, universally, relations stop nowhere' for the artist; 'the continuity of things is the whole matter . . . of comedy and tragedy'.[2] But it is worth asking what Rochester understood and saw as 'politics', and what were his status and experience within the governing class of the Restoration.

In the later eighteenth century the historian Sir John Dalrymple unearthed the evidence to prove to his astonished contemporaries that some of the Whig politicians of the reign

[1] *Poems on Affairs of State*: *Augustan Satirical Verse, 1660-1714*, ed. G. de F. Lord and others, 7 vols. (1963-75).
[2] Preface to *Roderick Hudson*, reprinted in *The Art of the Novel*: *Critical Prefaces by Henry James*, ed. Richard P. Blackmur (1934), p. 5.

of Charles II, by Dalrymple's time revered as Whig patriots, had accepted pensions from Louis XIV in return for securing the interruption of Parliamentary supply. Amongst them was Algernon Sydney himself, the martyr to Stuart tyranny.[3] I have nothing up my sleeve as sensational as that, no suggestion that Rochester was in anyone's pocket, or was the secret author of this or that pamphlet. The evidence of Rochester's political concerns and engagements—to be found essentially in his own writings and not so far, I'm afraid, anywhere else—is appropriately pretty negative. When in a letter he mentions his 'politics', there is a strong suspicion that he is merely alluding to his view of current court intrigues rather than to what might be taken for 'affairs of state'.[4]

To think about Rochester in this regard, it is useful to reflect on who and what he was as a man in the society of his time, including what he was as John Wilmot, second Earl of Rochester and third Viscount Wilmot of Athlone, in the Irish peerage.[5] On his father's side, the Wilmots, the recent family history was almost entirely military. The grandfather, Charles Wilmot, had established himself from Oxfordshire gentry as a soldier under Essex in Ireland, had acquired Irish lands and an Irish peerage as Viscount Wilmot, and was buried at Drogheda. His son Henry, Rochester's father, was also a soldier, and a very

---

[3] Sir John Dalrymple, *Memoirs of Great Britain and Ireland . . .*; 2 vols. (1771-3), Preface quoted by G.N. Clark, *The Later Stuarts* (1934, corrected edition 1940), p. 85n: 'When I found in the French dispatches Lord Russel intriguing with the court of Versailles, and Algernon Sidney taking money from it, I felt very near the same shock as if I had seen a son turn his back in the day of battle.'

[4] *The Letters of John Wilmot Earl of Rochester*, ed. Jeremy Treglown (1980), p. 189. Further references to this edition are given, where appropriate, after quotations in the text.

[5] The standard sources for Wilmot family history are *Dictionary of National Biography* and G. E. C[okayne], *Complete Peerage. . .* , ed. V. Gibbs and others, 14 vols. (1910-59).

successful one, serving under the Dutch in the 1630s, fighting in the Second Bishops' War against the Scots for Charles, again at Edgehill and Cropredy Bridge. Clarendon acknowledged his competence, though he didn't find him to his taste—he was bold, confident, hard-drinking, witty and popular with his troops. Comparing him with Goring, Clarendon admits that at least Wilmot 'never drank when he was within distance of an enemy', whilst Goring had been known to be drunk even in the thick of battle. He thought Goring had a better understanding 'except in the very exercise of debauchery, and then (Wilmot) was inspired', an interesting comment on the father of the son.[6] In the end, he got himself a permanent place in Stuart history, as the man who was with King Charles almost continuously during the flight from Worcester—on the run with his King taking risks in perfunctory disguise—and at last sailing with him from the Sussex coast to France. He was a close adviser of the young King in exile, and returned to England in secret in 1655 to take part in the abortive Royalist plots of that year, in which Henry Savile's mother Lady Savile was much involved. Perhaps at the same time he saw his son John, then aged about eight, but that is only a surmise. He died in Ghent in 1658, but his body was brought back to Oxfordshire later.

The Wilmots, Anglo-Irish and military in interest and reputation, provided young Rochester with no immediate links with the English establishment of influential families; for this, Rochester could look to his mother's family. Anne, Lady Rochester, was a St John, a family that from its lands at Lydiard Tregoze in Wiltshire had established influential connections by marriage in the pre-Civil War period. One branch was to become powerful in the Parliamentary and Cromwellian

---

[6] Clarendon, *History of the Rebellion* . . ., ed. W.D. Macray (1888), III, 388-90 and 444.

hierarchy. A sister of Lady Rochester had married a Villiers, a half-brother of the first duke of Buckingham. Another sister married an Apsley, a daughter of this marriage being Mrs Lucy Hutchinson. A third sister had a daughter who became the first wife of Edward Hyde, later Clarendon. The Villiers son, William, Lord Grandison, was a close friend of Hyde, and Grandison's daughter Barbara Villiers was later known to fame as Lady Castlemaine; it would not be apparent from Rochester's allusions to her that she was his first cousin once removed. It is easy to think these details of family connections rather tiresome antiquarian trivia, but it would be unwise to underestimate their significance for the life of the seventeenth-century ruling class, especially one emerging from the upheavals of Civil War, commonwealth and the restoration of the monarchy. Every family had, or needed, 'friends', the word 'friend' at that time usually meaning kin, however distant, who constituted a good part of the family 'interest'. Interest had to do with property, and influence. It also had to do with family honour, in a social system still based on honour, or shame, especially as regards the women, who linked honour to property and its prospects. The fact that Rochester's cousin, another Villiers, was seduced when young by the courtier Henry Jermyn did not endear that character to Rochester when he came to court.

What were some of the consequences of these connections for Rochester and his outlook? From the Wilmot side—and he was Lord Wilmot until he was ten years old—it might be possible to draw inferences about the son, but it is clear that Henry Wilmot could have had very little practical part in his son's upbringing.

More certainly Rochester received, and exploited, the full effects of being the son of the man to whom Charles personally owed so much. After leaving Wadham College, Rochester went abroad for three years with a tutor-companion, in France and

Italy. Returning to England in time for Christmas 1664 at the age of seventeen, he went straight to the court at Whitehall. It was the obvious place to go. True, he had a home with his mother in Oxfordshire, but the court was to be a second home, with the King a kind of second father at its head. Of the other court Wits, only Buckingham equalled Rochester in his sense of belonging to the royal court in a familial way from an early age, and Buckingham was of a different generation, older even than Charles himself. In due course Rochester was made one of the twelve gentlemen of the bedchamber, with an annual salary, in theory, of £1,000, and the duty of providing, as part of a rota, constant attendance on the King. Beneath him was an establishment of court officers and servants from the grooms of the bedchamber and the pages downwards. Above him, apart from the members of the royal family themselves, were only the four great officers of the court—the Lord Steward, the Lord Chamberlain, the Master of the Horse and the Vice Chamberlain.[7] Adding to the intensity of the experience, for a young man of Rochester's intelligence and sensibility, was the piquant fact that the reigning mistress, Lady Castlemaine, was his cousin.

One other figure about the court when Rochester arrived there, in it but not of it, was Clarendon the Lord Chancellor, a man now in his late fifties. And this brings us to the other side of the family, the St Johns. More than twenty years earlier, before Rochester was born, when Clarendon, then Edward Hyde, had to make his way from London to York to join the King before the Parliamentary authorities could prevent him, he made straight for Ditchley in Oxfordshire, the home of Anne, Lady Lee, as the woman who was to be Rochester's mother then was. He went to Ditchley because he knew Lady

[7] J.H. Wilson, *The Court Wits of the Restoration: An Introduction* (1948).

Lee well, as his sister-in-law, and also because he knew the road, Ditchley being not far from Great Tew (in the seventeenth century a traveller had to know the road). From Ditchley Clarendon got a friend over from Oxford to guide him by the backways to the north, the friend being William Chillingworth.[8] This is just one example of the usefulness to Clarendon of this family relationship. So it is not surprising that when Anne St John's son, Rochester, received the degree of MA at Oxford in September 1661 from the University Chancellor, Clarendon, he was greeted 'very affectionately'.[9]

Yet within three or four years Clarendon was registering his anger and dismay at the manners and outlook of the younger members of the families he respected most—Coventrys, Saviles, Falklands, Spencers, Villiers—whom he valued not only for their loyalty, but also for their intelligence and cultivation. Collectively this was a generation, who, as he put it, 'had never seen the King, and had been born and bred in those corrupt Times *when there was no King in Israel*'.[10] This was perhaps not strictly true of those born in the 1630s, but the general charge was valid: a generation of well-born war orphans, deprived and insecure at an early age, a not insignificant factor in the outlook and manners of the young aristocrats and higher gentry of the Restoration. For many of them, childhood had been marred: by their father's death in the wars—the Saviles, Spencers, Grandisons, Falklands (the younger Falkland was said, probably falsely, to have sold his father's library for a horse and a mare); by searches by Parliamentary troops and restless travel about England in search of safety; by the preponderant

---

[8] *The Life of Edward, Earl of Clarendon . . . Written By Himself* (1759), p. 60. Hereafter cited as *Continuation* (to 1667), separately paginated.
[9] Anthony à Wood, *Athenae Oxonienses*, (1692), II, 489.
[10] Clarendon, *Continuation*, p. 22.

influence of domestic chaplains and clerical guests, or by years abroad under socially inferior tutors, in the France of the Fronde. They formed a ready-made audience for Hobbes's *Leviathan* of 1651, a book said to have 'corrupted half the gentry of the nation'. The most distinguished war orphan of all was Charles II, who actually had Hobbes as a tutor. Hobbes would have been hurt to think that communicating his passion for geometry was corrupting. Yet there is not much doubt that his analysis of the nature of obligation, and his polemic against ecclesiastical authority and the interests of 'unpleasing priests' ('and those not onely amongst Catholiques, but even in that Church that hath presumed most of Reformation') spoke for the resentment and impatience which strained beneath the surface of many an Anglican and Royalist family.[11] Men of Rochester's and even Charles II's generation, unlike Clarendon, had few grounds for nostalgia about the blessings of Caroline peace.

Clarendon's lament for the passing of the old manners, written in 1672 after his fall, is very well known and often quoted: 'All Relations were confounded by the several Sects in Religion, which discountenanced all Forms of Reverence and Respect, as Reliques and Marks of Superstition . . .'.[12] More specifically he commented on the personal pressures at court, exerted by the younger courtiers, that contributed to his fall. He seems to have felt that his close friendship with his relative Grandison, the father of Lady Castlemaine, made him a special object of that lady's hatred:

> The Lady had Reason to hate him mortally, well knowing that there had been an inviolable Friendship between her Father and him to his Death . . . and that He was an

[11] Thomas Hobbes, *Leviathan*, chapter XII.
[12] Clarendon, *Continuation*, p. 21.

implacable Enemy to the Power and Interest She had with the King, and had used all the Endeavours He could to destroy it.[13]

It was generally acknowledged that the downfall of Clarendon was plotted, as Pepys put it, 'in my Lady Castlemaine's chamber'.[14]

No specific comment survives from Clarendon about Rochester himself, but one may be sure that he was included in the general commination. Comment does survive, however, about Rochester's friends the Saviles. When a proposal was floated in 1665 by the Duke of York, that the elder Savile, George (later Halifax), should be raised from baronet to the peerage, Clarendon objected 'with his usual Freedom'. The Duke said that Sir George 'had one of the best Fortunes of any Man in *England*, and lived the most like a great Man; that He had been very civil to him and his Wife in the North'. To this Clarendon replied that 'Sir *George Savile* was a Man of very ill-Reputation amongst Men of Piety and Religion, and was looked upon as void of all Sense of Religion, even to the doubting if not denying that there is a God, and that He was not reserved in any Company to publish his Opinions'.[15] Savile did get his peerage, as Viscount Halifax, but he had to wait another two years, until after Clarendon had gone.

When this comment on Halifax in his younger days is remembered, and when we add to it Burnet's report that in his last illness Rochester had said that Halifax was 'the Man in the World he valu'd most', it is permissible to doubt whether the usual construction put on Halifax's enjoining caution, in his

[13] ibid., p. 170.
[14] Samuel Pepys, *Diary*, 27 August 1667.
[15] Clarendon, *Continuation*, p. 297.

advice to Burnet about his task of writing an account of
Rochester, is the right one.[16]

As for the other Savile, the Duke had attached Henry to
himself as gentleman of the bedchamber, who, said Clarendon,
'being a young Man of Wit, and incredible Confidence and
Presumption, omitted no Occasion to vent his Malice against
the Chancellor, with a Licence that in former Times would
have been very penal'.[17]

It needs to be said of Clarendon that he directed his criticism
as well at characters like Henry Bennet, later Earl of Arlington,
the man at whose mansion of Euston, in Essex, amidst what
Evelyn described as pagan festivities, Charles was first 'bedded'
with Louise de Kéroualle, the Duchess of Portsmouth.
Arlington he regarded as a cynical and mercenary politician,
who, he said, 'knew no more of the Constitution and Laws of
England than He did of *China*, nor had in Truth a Care or
Tenderness for Church or State, but believed *France* was the
best Pattern in the World'.[18]

We are getting a little closer to 'politics'. Clarendon was an
accurate prophet. He knew the King's mind and disposition,
and he knew that the combination of Catholics, Dissenters and
courtiers that pulled him down opened the way to the
encroachments of French political and religious aggrandize-
ment. It is one of the ironies of the period that before many
years we find the more acute of the younger men, their eyes
opened to the facts of European politics, taking up a position
much like Clarendon's, both as regards the constitution at
home and the threat of France abroad. This is certainly explicit

[16] Gilbert Burnet to Halifax, 29 July 1680 in H.C. Foxcroft, 'Some Unpublished
Letters of Gilbert Burnet', *Camden Miscellany,* 11 (1907), 42 (Publications of
the Royal Historical Society).
[17] Clarendon, *Continuation,* p. 299.
[18] ibid., p. 184. *The Diary of John Evelyn,* ed. E.S. de Beer (1955), III, 589-90.

in the letters of Henry Savile to his brother, and from what little evidence there is it seems certain that by the late 1670s Rochester's view of Louis and his ambitions was deeply hostile. Yet others of the same background, like Robert Spencer, Earl of Sunderland, committed themselves to a largely Francophile foreign policy and what might be called a Gallic view of English government and administration.[19]

Rochester's own position was in certain important respects distinctive. He became a courtier, in the full sense of the word, his duty as far as he fulfilled it to serve personally the man he called his master. His public experience was intensely centred on the court and that outlying arena of court interest, the theatre; he seems to have had very little consciousness or experience of the city, which is markedly absent, either in allusion or attack, from his satires. He also made a few extraordinarily vigorous, successful and intrepid excursions into warfare, with the Fleet. It is worth remarking how energetically a whole court-based group, many of them from families which had suffered so much loss of life during the Civil War, committed themselves to the fighting at sea in the 1660s and early 1670s.

On the other hand, although a nobleman with a modest estate and fortune, mainly through marriage and royal bounty, Rochester had no 'interest'. Henry Wilmot's influence was a product of war, and personal service to the Crown. He had no great interest to pass on to his son. By comparison with the great men, not all of them peers, who from their estates in the provinces could if they wished exercise power at the centre, especially in times of crisis, the Wilmots's political weight was insignificant. In recommending George Savile for a peerage, the Duke of York urged, as was to be expected, 'the great

[19] J.P. Kenyon, *Robert Spencer Earl of Sunderland 1641-1702* (1958), pp. 84-6.

Interest that Sir *George Savile* had in the Northern Parts'.[20]
Interest was what counted. If one looks through the names of
the seven men who signed the invitation to William on 30 June
1688, on behalf of what they claimed was nineteen-twentieths
of the nation—names like Shrewsbury (a Talbot), Devonshire
(a Cavendish), Sidney, Danby, Lumley, mostly based north of
the Trent[21]—one finds they nearly all represent this stable
structure of interlocking financial and political interest in their
parts of England, a structure which was the basis of such
political stability as was achieved by the end of the century.
Grenville and Seymour in the west were similarly powerful at
that juncture.

Simply as a peer, and a relatively modest one in these terms,
Rochester was wholly dependent on court favour, the with-
drawal of which, or the fear of it, caused him feelings of panic
he could not disguise. Without the backing of interest which a
nobleman might look for, he felt all the strains of the feuding
and family-like hatreds of the court, lacking the compensating
independence of the need for court influence that was enjoyed
by some of his peers. Sunderland, chronically in debt and a
gambler, shows the same strains and desperate concern about
standing, in his very different career, without Rochester's own
distinctive resource of intellectual independence. So, for
Sunderland, politics must be made to pay; they might be made,
in a characteristic phrase, 'a good thing'.[22]

Rochester's dissociation from this kind of careerism was
total. He could write to his wife with mock formality of his

---

[20] Clarendon, *Continuation,* p. 298.
[21] *English Historical Documents 1660-1714,* ed. Andrew Browning (1953),
pp. 120-2.
[22] Sunderland to Lawrence Hyde, Earl of Rochester, 20 June 1683: '. . . to
persuade you from retiring at a time that business is likely to be as good a thing as
it can ever be.' Kenyon, *Sunderland,* p. 94.

being forced to stay at court 'till I had contriv'd a supply' (*Letters,* p. 80), or in plainer terms could confess that 'ready Cash I have but little, 'tis hard to come by' (p. 140), but the temptation of political opportunism he seems to have found easy to resist. His contempt for court politics informed the correspondence with Savile with a special sense of their belonging to a world apart, where the discourse of friends fell into the familiar style of like minds—'the style of business I am not versed in' (p. 229). Business was 'impertinent'. 'The meane Pollicy of Court prudence' destroyed trust—'makes us lye to one another all day, for feare of being betray'd by each other att night' (p. 67). In another letter he remarks that 'they who would be great in our little government seem as ridiculous to me as schoolboys who with much endeavour and some danger climb a crab-tree, venturing their necks for fruit which solid pigs would disdain if they were not starving' (p. 119). The 'stile politicall' is fit only for parody, and when he refers to the 'cabinet' he really means the women and pimps who sup with the King (p. 189). One is reminded of Halifax's ironic remark about the usefulness of a royal mistress 'in the immediate hours of her ministry'.[23] His most serious advice about affairs of state is given to Nell Gwynn, whom Rochester seems to have thought of as a more honest and useful member of the commonweal than any statesman:

> . . . my advice to the lady you wot of has ever been this: take your measures just contrary to your rivals; live in peace with all the world and easily with the King; never be so ill-natured to stir up his anger against others, but let

[23] Halifax, *A Character of King Charles II,* in *Life and Letters of Sir George Savile, First Marquis of Halifax . . . with a new edition of his Works,* ed. H.C. Fox-croft (1898), II, 349.

> him forget the use of a passion which is never to do you
> good; cherish his love wherever it inclines, and be assured
> you can't commit greater folly than pretending to be
> jealous; but on the contrary, with hand, body, head, heart
> and all the faculties you have, contribute to his pleasure all
> you can and comply with his desires throughout. (p. 189)

This has something in common (but only something) with
Saint Evremond's advice to the Duchesse Mazarin's page Dery,
that for the sake of his future as a singer at court, where he is
'caressed by Duchesses', he should submit to being 'sweetened
by a gentle Operation'.[24] Rochester and Saint Evremond both
understood the world of the great in terms of loves and hates,
pleasure and pain, but Rochester's cynicism and hedonism are
more implicitly subtle and serious. Here, he is saying, is
proposed a real offering to the good of a prince and therefore to
the peace of the court.

In the last year of his life, when the ruthless manipulation of
the Popish Plot was at its height, Rochester summed up, and
wrote off, the whole political scene, from the point of view of
the privileged irresponsibility of the true courtier:

> The general heads under which this whole island may be
> considered are spies, beggars and rebels. The trans-
> positions and mixtures of these make an agreeable variety:
> busy fools and cautious knaves are bred out of them and
> set off wonderfully, though of this latter sort we have
> fewer now than ever, hypocrisy being the only vice in
> decay amongst us. Few men here dissemble their being
> rascals and no woman disowns being a whore. (p. 232)

---

[24] *The Letters of Saint Evremond,* ed. John Hayward (1930), p. 267. *The Works*
. . . translated by Des Maizeaux, second edn (1728), II, 331.

It is not difficult to find parallels in the comments of other court wits. Two years after Rochester's death Sedley wrote to Chesterfield:

> . . . Whigg and Tory . . . are in my opinion (at least the violent part on both sides) much of the same stuff at bottom since they are so easily converted one to another, I mean self interest; for instance the Lord Sunderland upon the Dutchess of Portsmouth's arrival is received at Court [one year previously he had been a violent driver for Exclusion; now he makes terms through Portsmouth.] The Lord Vaughan is this week to be marryd to the Lady Ann Savile notwithstanding he having voted her father an enemy to King and country last Sessions. Tho wee are not blest with Poets that can write us comedys equall to the auntients, I beleive never was an age so comical as this . . .[25]

A little earlier Sackville's ballad 'My Opinion' had opened with the verse:

> After thinking this fortnight of Whig and of Tory,
> This to me is the long and the short of the story:
> They are all fools or knaves, and they keep up this pother
> On both sides, designing to cheat one another.[26]

And Mulgrave, in his notorious *Essay Upon Satire* (1679), had mocked the 'busy man', the wit turned statesman who 'forfeits

[25] Sir Charles Sedley to the Earl of Chesterfield, August 1682. In V. de Sola Pinto, *Sir Charles Sedley 1639-1701* (1927), p. 152.
[26] *Poems on Affairs of State: Volume 2: 1678-1681*, ed. Elias F. Mengel, Jr. (1965), p. 391.

his friends, his freedom, and his fame'.[27] Examples of this scorn
for the life of politics are countless, but in Rochester's case
what might be called the purity of the sentiment is exceptional.
Sackville and Mulgrave became Privy Councillors, Sedley an
MP. Even his dear friend Savile, who as a younger son had to
make his way up the ladder of office, could be gently twitted as a
'statesman'. In the common 'bitchery' of court talk malicious
comparisons were no doubt made, but Rochester disclaimed
political envy; he was, he said, 'not at all stung with my Lord
M[ulgrave]'s mean ambition' (p. 119). We might almost be
listening to Donne: 'Take you a course, get you a place. . .'.

Rochester's personal history, and the special intensities of
his life at court, where he was so close to government and yet so
deliberately apart from it, help to explain, I think, why his
distinction as a satirist is not in any important sense a product
of political understanding or engagement; at least it is clear
that in his satires politics were subjected to a highly personal
focus. His 'Sceptre' lampoon on Charles II is written with the
insolence of innermost court privilege, a *lèse-majesté* beyond
politics. At the other extreme his lines on the upright statesman
and churchman in *A Satyr against Reason and Mankind* open
up an ethical generality and scope well above the factional view
of so much Restoration political satire. The intervening space
was at best occupied by polemicists who, like Marvell, spoke up
for the political nation at large:

> When the sword glitters o'er the judges head,
> And fear has coward churchmen silenced,

[27] *Poems on Affairs of State: Volume 1: 1660-1678*, ed. George de F. Lord
(1963), pp. 407-8. Also in *Anthology of Poems on Affairs of State* . . . ed. George
de F. Lord (1975), p. 190.

Then is the poet's time, 'tis then he draws,
And single fights forsaken Virtue's cause.[28]

The radical indignation of a poem such as 'The History of
Insipids' (1674)—so long attributed to Rochester but now
thought to be by John Freke—implies an alternative political
order, and the means to attain it, with which his intensely
personal engagements had little to do.[29] Rochester's response
to a letter from Savile about the 'great marriage' of William of
Orange to Princess Mary (1677) was a characteristically
hilarious fantasy, his version of a 'sober advice':

> I wish the King were soberly advised about a main
> advantage in this marriage which may possibly be omitted:
> I mean the ridding his Kingdom of some old beauties and
> young deformities who swarm and are a grievance to his
> liege people. A foreign prince ought to behave himself like
> a kite, who is allowed to take one royal chick for his reward
> but then 'tis expected before he leaves the country his
> flock shall clear the whole parish of all the garbage and
> carrion many miles about. The King had never such an
> opportunity, for the Dutch are very foul feeders . . .
> (pp. 166-7).

His 'a foreign prince ought to behave himself like a kite', simply
thrown off in a letter, anticipates Swift by twenty years.

The historian Gilbert Burnet and modern authorities such as
Andrew Browning and David Ogg variously locate the precise
emergence of country and court parties in the early 1670s,
years which saw the virtual disappearance of the unattached

[28] Andrew Marvell, 'Tom May's Death', lines 63-6.
[29] For the attribution to the republican John Freke see Frank H. Ellis, 'John Freke
and *The History of Insipids*', *Philological Quarterly,* 44 (1965), 472-83.

member of the Commons.[30] Any conclusions about the
consequences of these party alignments for personal relations,
within the tightly-knit society at the top, are bound to be
speculative. But there is not much doubt that the corruption of
social intercourse by political differences, for which there is
evidence, was felt by Rochester as a real evil. With whatever
obvious qualifications, we may say that in this respect he
belonged to the same culture as Clarendon, and that in their
very different ways they shared a distaste for the new political
scene. Like many cultivated Restoration noblemen, Clarendon
was devoted to Tacitus, and perhaps Rochester was too; he
certainly read Livy.[31] They might both have quoted Tacitus on
the Rome of the ageing Augustus, soon to be Tiberius's Rome:
'igitur verso civitatis statu nihil usquam prisci et integri
moris'—'so it was a changed world, and of the old soundness of
manners nothing remained'.[32] Rochester survived just long
enough to know the new world of mass lobbying by petition, of
party management and political clubs and lists of men 'worthy'
and 'unworthy', of spies, informers, and Mr Oates: a politicized
society to which one answer was 'that second bottle Harry . . .
the sincerest, wisest, & most impartiall downright freind we
have' (p. 67). Rochester would perhaps not have dissented from
the ideal of conversation celebrated by Dryden, in a dedication
addressed to their mutual friend Sedley (himself the enemy of
those who disputed state affairs 'with more Heat, Concern, and
Animosity' than was consistent with good humour): 'our genial
nights, where our discourse is neither too serious, nor too light,

[30] Gilbert Burnet, *History of My Own Time: Part I, The Reign of Charles the
Second*, ed. Osmund Airy (1900), I, 486. Andrew Browning, *Thomas Osborne
Earl of Danby and Duke of Leeds 1632-1712* (1951), I, 173. David Ogg, *England
in the Reign of Charles II* (2nd edn corrected, 1963), II, 526-7.
[31] Treglown, *Rochester's Letters*, p. 117.
[32] Tacitus, *Annals*, I.iv.

but always pleasant, and for the most part instructive: the raillery neither too sharp upon the present, nor too censorious on the absent'. The rest of the sentence—'and the cups only such as will raise the conversation of the night, without disturbing the business of the morrow'—he might have thought priggish.[33]

A foreign visitor was witness to the inhibiting effects of politics on conversation. The Italian adventurer and gossip-monger Gregorio Leti visited England in the 1680s, and wrote an account of what he found, in his *Del Teatro Brittanico* (1683). He was an acceptable dinner guest for his stock of scabrous anecdote about Roman cardinals. At one dinner party of great men, he remarked that he intended writing a book about English affairs, whereupon 'one of the guests said that I had to be careful because there were intricate and difficult matters to disentangle; a milord added that if I were he I would be careful in speaking about the King or about Parliament or the Duke of York . . . one advised me not to talk about this, or about that, so that when all was said, nothing was left to speak about, but the hire of boatmen, or of coachmen.'[34] Of another conversation at table of the period, a correspondent wrote: 'there was a spiteful dialogue . . . neither spared each other, nor anybody else. Your name came up.'[35]

When Rochester was dying, John Locke was already at work

---

[33] John Dryden, Dedication to Sir Charles Sedley prefixed to *The Assignation* (1673), in *Of Dramatic Poesy and Other Critical Essays*, ed. George Watson (1962), I, 186. Sedley's 'Essay on Entertainments', briefly quoted in the text, was first printed in his *Miscellaneous Works* (1702). *Poetical and Dramatic Works,* ed. V. de S. Pinto (1928), II, 98-9.

[34] Gregorio Leti, *Del Teatro Brittanico* (1683), I, 45-6: '. . . che mi consigliava à non parlar di questo, un'altro à non parlar di quello, di modo che raccolti tutti insieme questi pareri, altro non restava da parlare che dal nolo de' Barcarvoli, ò di quello de' Cocchieri.'

[35] Hist. MSS Com. *Downshire*, I (i), 213.

on the manuscript of his *Two Treatises of Government*, published after the Revolution. Two more contrasted minds in the consideration of affairs of state it would be difficult to find, the poet-rake and the ideologue of liberal politics, whose language and axioms were to shape the aspirations of millions. Contrasts such as this give the age of Charles II its peculiar rough poignancy. Locke's new discourse was about the ends of government and the rights of property. Rochester's idiom was formed by codes and habits fast becoming archaic. His state was in the hand of kings, good or bad, their courts arenas for the rituals of power, where sexual conquest and the constraints of patronage were interchangeable in description. To the military Royalism of the Wilmots was added a reading of Hobbes and the service of the 'lewdest Prince'. A dialogue between Rochester and Locke, on government, in the 1670s? Physically, it was possible; conceptually, it is hard to imagine.

Wanton Expressions

DAVID TROTTER

What is the paradox that Rochester, at a famous moment in *A Satyr against Reason and Mankind*, offers to recant? There is, from a certain point of view, apparent contradiction in an intelligent man's flattery of dumb beasts. But the *Satyr*, the most purely exasperated poem in the language, can hardly be thought to hang on this or any other puzzle. Take it away, and Rochester hasn't conceded much. Yet he says it emphatically:

> If upon earth there dwell such God-like men,
> I'll here recant my paradox to them,
> Adore those shrines of virtue, homage pay,
> And, with the rabble world, their laws obey.

Whatever the paradox may be, recanting it would seem to involve submission to the conventional morality which governs the rabble world: a fiercely resented gesture. One conundrum more or less would surely not make that kind of difference. A reputation, at the very least, has been laid on the line.

Could it be that Rochester thought his poem paradoxical not in the sense that it bred philosophical puzzles, but in the sense that it defied the *doxa* (or accepted wisdom) of the age? This is a sense of the term less familiar today than it would have been to

111

someone like Thomas Hobbes, whose definition was formulated in response to a polemic by Bishop Bramhall:

> The Bishop speaks often of paradoxes with such scorn or detestation, that a simple reader would take a paradox either for felony or some other heinous crime, or else for some ridiculous turpitude; whereas perhaps a judicious reader knows what the word signifies; and that a paradox, is an opinion not yet generally received.[1]

The *Satyr* also puts forward an opinion not yet generally received, which the guardians of *doxa* might well have considered a political threat. Rochester, too, had his problems with 'prelatic pride'. In this sense, the whole poem is a para-dox; and recanting it would have involved a most uncharacteristic act of conformity.

Rochester was in an even worse position than Hobbes. He had to contend with *would-be* bishops. On 24 February 1675, Edward Stillingfleet, then thirty-nine years old and a royal chaplain, preached before the King a sermon which alluded disparagingly to Rochester's *Satyr*. Pointing this out, Kristoffer Paulson has suggested that the 'epilogue' to the *Satyr* was written as a reply to Stillingfleet's attack.[2] It does, after all, criticize the kind of churchman

> Whose envious heart makes preaching a pretence,
> With his obstreperous, saucy eloquence,
> To chide at kings, and rail at men of sense . . .

[1] Thomas Hobbes, *English Works,* ed. W. Molesworth (1839-45), V, 304. Dustin Griffin notes this sense of the term, but doesn't develop its political implications: *Satires Against Men: The Poems of Rochester* (1973), p. 200.
[2] Kristoffer Paulson, 'The Reverend Edward Stillingfleet and the "Epilogue" to Rochester's *A Satyr against Reason and Mankind*', *Philological Quarterly*, 50, (1971), 657-63.

Furthermore, if we follow Paulson and accept the alternative reading of 'Stillingfleet's replies' for 'Sibbes' soliloquies' in line 74 of the poem, we discover a reason for the royal chaplain's hostility.

Vieth prints 'Sibbes' soliloquies', but has to depart from his copy-text in order to do so. It seems symptomatic of our thinking about Rochester that the most accessible modern edition of his poems should suppose him to be satirizing a long-dead Puritan enthusiast rather than a contemporary reformer whose career was taking shape in front of his very eyes; taking shape, moreover, in an age when the control of public opinion was vested in such careers, and had been ever since Elizabeth talked of tuning her pulpits. I want to suggest here that there was a political aspect to Rochester's wit, and that his greatest poem was generated not simply out of inner turmoil, but also out of the tension between points of view in society.

For Stillingfleet was no isolated fanatic. His allegiance lay with the Latitudinarian party in the Church of England, whose aim was to promote a rational religion favourable to the increase of trade, empire and science.[3] He stood with men like John Tillotson, Isaac Barrow, John Wilkins, Joseph Glanvill, Robert Boyle and Thomas Sprat. One of the moralists attacked by the *Satyr*, Simon Patrick, was the author of the book which had first identified this movement, *A Brief Account of the New Sect of Latitude-Men* (1662). During the 1660s and 1670s, the latitude-men gradually won their way to preferment and influence. By latitude, they meant burying differences for long enough to furnish a society developing from civil war to empire

---

[3] For accounts of Latitudinarian ideology, see Richard B. Schlatter, *The Social Ideas of Religious Leaders, 1660-1688* (1940); Barbara J. Shapiro, 'Latitudinarianism and Science in Seventeenth-Century England', in *The Intellectual Revolution of the Seventeenth Century*, ed. Charles Webster (1974); Margaret C. Jacob, *The Newtonians and the English Revolution, 1689-1720* (1976).

with spiritual and intellectual consensus: in short, with *doxa*. And on occasion their vigorous expounding of *doxa* brought them up against such examples of the unreformed as the Earl of Rochester, a longitude-man if ever there was one.

Two points need to be made here about their view of society. They were, in the first place, much concerned with habits of speech. By this I mean not only the Royal Society's project for a 'real language' which would relate words to things, but also a more practical understanding of the forms of address used by men and women in society: in pulpit, law court, exchange, home and coffee house. Social stability was thought to depend to some extent on the way people spoke to each other. In the second place, the latitude-men advocated, both in behaviour and in speech, a certain diffidence: the suppression of anything which might give rise to unnecessary conflict. It was a doctrine of appeasement; or rather of appeasement among ourselves, but aggression towards mute nature (and, where they were to be found, babbling natives). 'I love to speak of Persons with Civility,' Boyle wrote, 'but of Things with Freedom.'[4]

Political stability seemed real enough to Stillingfleet, preaching in 1678:

> That is certainly the happiest condition of a People, where the Prince sits upon the Throne of Majesty and Power, doing righteousness and shewing kindness; and the People sit *every man under his Vine, and under his Fig-tree,* enjoying the fruits of his own labours, or his Ancestor's bounty . . .

All would be well, except that you could never be quite sure what the subjects of Charles II were getting up to under their

[4] Robert Boyle, *Certain Physiological Essays* (1661), p. 26.

vines and fig trees. The political achievement was being undermined by a lack of social discipline:

> But what can we say to that looseness and debauchery of manners, to that riot and luxury, to that wantonness and prophaneness, to that fashion of customary swearing, and *Atheistick Drollery*, which have been so much and so justly complained of among us?[5]

If available in sufficient quantities, and cunningly directed, such indiscipline might well pose a political threat. The solution was to stamp out customary swearing and atheistic drollery while they remained a mere sport, something to while away the long hours under vine and fig tree.

During the Interregnum, the habit of casual swearing had become associated with Cavaliers on one hand, and Ranters on the other. The former were popularly known as 'Dammees': in January 1653, the fact that a sailor had been heard to 'swear two or three times by his Maker without any provocation' was taken to prove that he was a Royalist.[6] The latter swore as a gesture of contempt for established religion, and when Parliament moved against them it was by means of 'An Act for the better preventing of prophane Swearing and Cursing' (28 June 1650). After the Restoration, the idle rich and the radical sects continued to be spoken of, almost in the same breath, as the enemies of society. To Stillingfleet, rakes were '*Zealots* in wickedness'. Rakes and enthusiasts had become, Glanvill thought, the main source of contempt for the clergy: 'We are gone over as the stones in the street, by the *carnal* proud, and reckon'd as the dirt of it by the *spiritual* Scorners'.

[5] Edward Stillingfleet, *Works* (1710), I, 245.
[6] Christopher Hill, *Society and Puritanism in Pre-Revolutionary England* (1969), p. 406.

Clement Ellis reported in 1660 that people had given the name
'*Sparke* or *Raunter*' to gallants.[7]

By now, though, it was the gallants (the 'Damn-me-blades',
in Bunyan's expression) who did most of the swearing.
According to Glanvill, religious fanatics confirm 'with *sighs*
and solemn *nods*' slanders which the rakes have already
broadcast 'with *Oaths* and *Dammee's*'. If anything, it was the
latter habit which seemed most offensive, and which drew
down the wrath of Glanvill's colleagues. Boyle, in a polemic
written in 1647 but not published until 1695, held oaths
responsible for the bitterness of the Civil War. Tillotson
thought 'Vices of the Tongue' so prevalent and so harmful that
he collected Isaac Barrow's sermons on the subject into a single
volume and published them in 1678. Barrow had devoted a
whole sermon, and much incidental comment, to the vice of
casual swearing. Tillotson himself, preaching in 1681,
launched an attack on 'the great Sin of *Swearing in common
conversation*, upon trivial and needless occasions'.[8]

They weren't the only ones to feel nervous. Some dissenters
also campaigned against swearing, while the agony columns of
the day insisted with threadbare sarcasm that Damn-me-blades
must have been born with mouths at the wrong end of their
bodies.[9] But the latitude-men had more precise objections.

[7] Stillingfleet, *Works*, I, 116; Joseph Glanvill, *Seasonable Reflections and
Discourses in order to the Conviction, & Cure of the Scoffing, & Infidelity of a
Degenerate Age* (1676), p. 89; Clement Ellis, *The Gentile Sinner, or, England's
Brave Gentleman Characteriz'd* (1660), p. 11.
[8] Glanvill, *Seasonable Reflections*, p. 69; Boyle, *A Free Discourse against
Customary Swearing* (1695), pp. 12-13; Isaac Barrow, *Several Sermons against
Evil-Speaking* (1678); John Tillotson, *Works* (3rd edn, 1721), p. 246.
[9] See, for example, Richard Baxter, *A Treatise of Self-Deniall* (1675), p. 144;
John Bunyan, *Works,* ed. George Offor (1853), III, 601-5; Daniel Defoe, *An
Essay upon Projects* (1697), p. 240; Ellis, *Gentile Sinner*, p. 36; Josiah Dare,
Counsellor Manners His Last Legacy to His Son (1673), p. 18.

Oaths, Barrow said, are 'wast and insignificant words', 'meer excrescencies of Speech', surplus to semantic requirements. What they encode is not information, but the attitude of a speaker who is out to bully or provoke or show off. Casual swearing, Tillotson thought, 'is so far from adorning and filling a man's discourse, that it makes it look swoln and bloated, and more bold and blustring, than becomes persons of gentle and good breeding'. People fall back on oaths, another writer complained, when they have run out of arguments: then 'whole vollies' are 'discharged upon the doubtful'. As long as such practices remained fashionable there was small chance of sober and pragmatic communication among men in society. After all, Barrow wondered, 'if men are wont to dally with Swearing every-where, can they be expected to be strict and serious therein at the Bar, or in the Church?'[10]

Swearing touched another nerve. It seemed a peculiarly gratuitous sin. 'I do not like this doing in jest,' Boyle wrote, 'what a man may be damn'd for in earnest.' Tillotson agreed: 'Profit or Pleasure there is none in it, nor any thing in mens natural tempers to incite them to it.'[11] Swearing satisfied no need, and brought no reward; it thoroughly violated the ethic of 'sober self-love' which the latitude-men had put their faith in. How could you trust someone who gratuitously sacrificed his mortal soul with every other word he spoke? That, indeed, was sinning for the hell of it.

In an atmosphere of this sort a man could be identified politically as much by the way he spoke as by what he said. So it is hardly surprising that another Latitudinarian, Gilbert Burnet, should congratulate himself on having dissuaded Rochester

---

[10] Barrow, *Several Sermons*, pp. 32 and 30; Tillotson, *Works*, p. 247; Richard Allestree, *The Government of the Tongue* (1674), p. 200.
[11] Boyle, *Free Discourse,* p. 58; Tillotson, *Works*, p. 247.

from swearing: 'an ill habit grown so much upon him, that he could hardly govern himself, when he was any ways heated, three Minutes without falling into it'.[12] The notorious rake had to be seen to have repented not only of his dissolute behaviour, but also of his foul speech. By the same token, that speech would have marked him during his life as an enemy of the latitude-men.

Which doesn't tell us much about Rochester's poetry. But he was primarily a satirist, and the contemporary vogue for scabrous lampooning posed exactly the same kind of threat as the 'ill habit' of swearing. It, too, was gratuitous and provocative. 'Satyrical virulency may vex men sorely,' Barrow said, 'but it hardly ever soundly converts them.'[13] In social and political terms, there wasn't much to choose between customary swearing and customary lampooning; unless, of course, you could remove the element of gratuitousness from satire, without emasculating it altogether. This is something Dryden attempted, in theory if not in practice. The letter he wrote to Rochester in 1673 shows him already aware of the problem. His observations about the Duke of Buckingham, he says, 'would easily run into lampoon, if I had not forsworn that dangerous part of wit'.[14] He knew that lampoons tended to provoke without reforming, and had clearly decided to keep his head down below the parapet.

Subsequently, of course, Dryden was to disregard his own advice, but the dangers inherent in satirical virulence remained at the front of his mind twenty years later, when he came to write his *Discourse concerning the Original and Progress of*

[12] Gilbert Burnet, *Some Passages of the Life and Death of John, Earl of Rochester* (1680), in *Rochester: The Critical Heritage,* ed. D. Farley-Hills (1972), p. 85.
[13] Barrow, *Several Sermons,* p. 158.
[14] John Dryden, *Letters,* ed. Charles E. Ward (1942), pp. 9-10.

Satire, although by then it was the dangers to society rather than to self which preoccupied him. The *Discourse* was dedicated to the Earl of Dorset, and begins by commending that nobleman's transcendence of faction. The compliment is implausible, but it states a major theme of the essay: the need for diffidence and appeasement. ''Tis incident to an elevated understanding, like your Lordship's, to find out the errors of other men: but 'tis your prerogative to pardon them.'[15]

The same could be said of Dorset's poetry: 'There is more of salt in all your verses than I have seen in any of the Moderns, or even of the Ancients; but you have been sparing of the gall, by which means you have pleased all readers, and offended none' (II, 75). Dryden is taking issue with Rochester's description of Dorset as 'The best good man, with the worst-natur'd Muse'. This remark, he says, is typical of Rochester's 'self-sufficiency': 'an insolent, sparing, and invidious panegyric'. Rochester, we are made to feel, injected more gall than salt into *his* judgements. The contrast between the two noblemen is lightly sketched, but nonetheless emphatic; and it is the model of inoffensive severity provided by Dorset which we carry forward into our reading of Dryden's essay.

The model becomes evident when Dryden tries to dissociate Roman satire from the 'invective poems' of the Greeks (II, 103); or when he complains that Persius 'rather insulted over vice and folly, than exposed them' (II, 119). He is clearly concerned about the havoc wrought by invective poems: 'In a word, that former sort of satire, which is known in England by the name of lampoon, is a dangerous sort of weapon, and for the most part unlawful. We have no moral right to the reputation

---

[15] Dryden, *Of Dramatic Poesy and Other Critical Essays,* ed. G. Watson (1962), II, 74. Further references to Dryden's critical essays here are incorporated into the text.

of other men' (II, 125). It is a concern Rochester never shared, and the remark about Persius could no doubt be applied to him as well.

The model is also evident in the form of the *Discourse*. The comparison between the three Roman satirists has always been distorted, Dryden says, by the 'partiality of mankind', each expert preferring the poet in whose works he is expert. It is rather like the Roman circus, where support for a particular team of charioteers, however fortuitous at the outset, rapidly became a creed, 'and that so earnestly, that disputes and quarrels, animosities, commotions, and bloodshed, often happened' (II, 117). Dryden, like Dorset, must somehow rise above faction.

He had done so in his *Essay of Dramatic Poesy* by imitating the 'modest inquisitions' of the Royal Society (I, 123). The scientists sometimes adopted tentative and exploratory forms like the essay or the 'conference' among gentlemen, using— Glanvill said—'*so much caution* in our disquisitions, that we do not *suddenly* give *firm* assents to things not well understood, or *examin'd*'.[16] Dryden's *Discourse*, like the earlier *Essay*, could hardly be accused of suddenly giving firm assent to things not well understood. 'To come to a conclusion. . . .' he promises airily at one point; but twenty pages later he still hasn't quite got round to it. The true scientist, Boyle had written, should speak 'doubtingly' and use expressions like '*Perhaps, It seems, 'Tis not improbable*'. He should conceive 'warily', Glanvill confirmed, and speak 'with as much *caution* and *reserve*, in the humble Forms of (*So I think*, and *In my opinion*, and *Perhaps 'tis so*—) with great defference to opposite Perswasion'.[17] And

---

[16] Glanvill, *Philosophia Pia; or a Discourse of the Religious Temper, and Tendencies of the Experimental Philosophy* (1671), p. 71.
[17] Boyle, *Certain Physiological Essays,* p. 16; Glanvill, *Plus Ultra* (1668), p. 147.

Dryden certainly peppered the *Discourse* with 'humble Forms' of this kind.

But it is the passage on 'fine raillery', Dryden's fullest account of the purpose of satire, which reveals the extent of his flirtation with Latitudinarian principles. 'He that can bear a friendly touch,' Barrow thought, 'will not endure to be lashed with angry and reproachful words.' So even if we have occasion to rebuke someone, we should not employ offensive language ('calling him a Liar, a Deceiver, a Fool').[18] The purpose of Dryden's fine raillery was also to criticize without provoking: 'How easy it is to call rogue and villain, and that wittily! But how hard to make a man appear a fool, a blockhead, or a knave, without using any of those opprobrious terms!' (II, 136-7). Fine raillery is the ultimate skill, and Dorset's 'particular talent'.

There can be no doubt that the latitude-men recognized in satire a threat to their reform of the nation's speech habits. 'Satyr and Invective,' Tillotson said,

> are the easiest kind of Wit. Almost any degree of it will serve to abuse and find fault. For Wit is a keen Instrument, and every one can cut and gash with it; but to carve a beautiful Image, and to polish it, requires great Art and dexterity.[19]

A noted satirist himself, Dryden could not afford such wholesale condemnation; the only 'Medall' he had ever carved did not lack for abuse and fault-finding. But Tillotson's distinction between clumsy invective and dexterous praise could be transposed into a distinction between types of satire, between offensive railing (Juvenal) and inoffensive rallying (Horace).

---

[18] Barrow, *Several Sermons*, pp. 154 and 139.
[19] Tillotson, *Sermons Preach'd upon Several Occasions* (1671), p. 123.

There is a vast difference, Dryden says, 'betwixt the slovenly butchering of a man, and the fineness of a stroke that separates the head from the body, and leaves it standing in its place' (II, 137). Both men wanted to avoid gratuitous violence—cutting and gashing—which they saw as evil in itself and a cause of unnecessary conflict.

Tillotson could speak of wit as a moral handicraft, but Dryden needed a slightly more robust image here: 'A man may be capable, as Jack Ketch's wife said of his servant, of a plain piece of work, a bare hanging; but to make a malefactor die sweetly was only belonging to her husband' (II, 137). Even so, Dryden didn't want to overdo the robustness, and congratulated himself on the delicacy he had shown in disposing of the Duke of Buckingham. 'If I had rallied, I might have suffered for it justly: but I managed my own work more happily, perhaps more dexterously.' The tough-guy attitude is put aside for a moment, and the executioner's touch becomes—happily, dexterously—a moral handicraft.

Twenty years earlier, Dryden was afraid to lampoon Buckingham. Then *Absalom and Achitophel* had done the deed, and now he wanted to disclaim any vicious intent. The *Discourse* reproduces this zigzag approach. At the first sign of trouble, Dryden could duck behind a parapet constructed of appeasing gestures and 'humble Forms'. Yet he was by no means a member of the Latitudinarian party, and political isolation had strengthened his instinctive preference for a virulent Juvenalian satire. He knew that the business of satire was to sort people out. Any reader of his previous work, or of the ensuing translations, would surely have noticed the discrepancy between theory and practice. But Dryden makes the right noises. He recants *his* paradox in advance, by the tribute to Dorset; and the frequent attacks on lampooning ensure that it stays recanted. In short, he registers a genuine ambivalence about the effect of satire, and this is something that Rochester, protected by rank and by more than a little 'self-sufficiency', would never do.

Thus, Dryden admits that revenge is a permissible motive for lampooning, but points out that an inability to forgive the sins of others is contrary to 'Christian charity' (II, 125). Although himself 'naturally vindicative', moral scruple has held him back. Rochester, on the other hand, told Burnet that a man could not write with life, 'unless he were heated by Revenge; For to make a *Satyre* without Resentments, upon the cold Notions of *Phylosophy*, was as if a man would in cold blood, cut men's throats who had never offended him'. He rejected the role of skilled executioner which Dryden was to adopt. 'And he said, the lies in these Libels came often in as Ornaments that could not be spared without spoiling the beauty of the *Poem*.'[20] So he rejected, too, the objective public criteria which determined when and where Jack Ketch was to practise his art, and which supposedly moralized Dryden's satire. It almost amounted to an aesthetic of gratuitousness: the more far-fetched the accusation, the better. This failure even to consider the justice or the effects of lampooning distinguished Rochester from Dryden, and set him on a collision course with *doxa*.

Dryden's talk of Jack Ketch had its serious side. He really did want to equip the satirist with an accountable public role, which would supersede the random dissemination of anony-mous lampoons via coffee houses. Hence, I think, his insistence that satire is a branch of heroic poetry. For the recognized role of the epic poet gave a kind of validity to his utterances, just as a pulpit sanctified the words spoken from it. If the satirist could be assimilated to that role, he might escape the charge of

[20] In Farley-Hills, *Critical Heritage,* p. 54.

gratuitous provocation so often levelled against him.

Rochester made no such effort. Or, rather, he wanted to find
a role for the satirist, but without abandoning the pleasures of
gratuitous provocation. *Timon* and *Tunbridge Wells* are as
much concerned with this problem as they are with any criticism
of society. In both poems, it is important that the satiric
protagonist should be seen as a victim; folly and vice represent
a perpetually renewed affront to his personal dignity, a cause
for resentment. Timon is seized in the Mall by an importunate
social climber and dragged off to dinner; since he does not want
to be there in the first place, he is free to respond violently. We
can't really tell whether the protagonist of *Tunbridge Wells*
wants to be there or not, but his trip is described as an ordeal
from the outset. Both men are felt to be on the receiving end of
some pretty heavy treatment. They do not so much act as—
'heated by Revenge'—re-act. And by the time each new affront
has been absorbed, it's too late to do anything about it—except
fume.

Or move on, which is what the protagonist of *Tunbridge
Wells* does, slipping hurriedly from one desperate scene to the
next, always, of course, to no avail:

> But often when one would Charybdis shun,
> Down upon Scylla 'tis one's fate to run,
> For here it was my cursèd luck to find
> As great a fop, though of another kind,
> A tall stiff fool that walked in Spanish guise:
> The buckram puppet never stirred its eyes,
> But grave as owl it looked, as woodcock wise.

The fop repels by his rigidity: like several other figures in the
poem, he is physically straitened, and afflicted by a kind of
semantic lockjaw. And what distinguishes the satirist from

these dummies is a certain fluidity of action and speech when all around him waddle or stutter. Invective allows him to steal a march on folly. As for vice, that doesn't really come into it. The dummies haven't the brains to sin, and a remark passed about the knight's retainers holds good generally:

> Nature has done the business of lampoon,
> And in their looks their characters has shown.

Where the business hasn't already been done by nature, it's been done by Shadwell or by Andrew Marvell. So there are few surprises. Clement Ellis, for one, knew the kind of fop Rochester was talking about: 'Sometimes he walks as if he went in a *Frame*, again as if both head and every member of him *turned* upon *Hinges*. Every step he takes present you with a perfect *Puppit-play*.'[21] The protagonist of *Tunbridge Wells* seems to have been presented with a whole series of such puppet plays, and his resentment of the experience is itself pure theatre. It performs a sense of grievance, never more so than in the plangent conclusion:

> Bless me! thought I, what thing is man, that thus
> In all his shapes, he is ridiculous?
> Ourselves with noise of reason we do please
> In vain: humanity's our worst disease.
> Thrice happy beasts are, who, because they be
> Of reason void, are so of foppery.
> Faith, I was so ashamed that with remorse
> I used the insolence to mount my horse;
> For he, doing only things fit for his nature,
> Did seem to me by much the wiser creature.

[21] Ellis, *Gentile Sinner,* p. 30.

The bold favouring of dumb beasts enables the speaker to avoid the problem of criteria, the moral effort of distinguishing between men. Remorse, here, achieves its literal sense of biting back: a physical reflex which performs the satirist's sense of grievance.

During the late 1660s and early 1670s the Latitudinarians mounted a campaign against such gratuitous jeering at traditional pieties. They preached on texts like Proverbs 14:9 ('Fools make a mock at sin') and 2 Peter 3:3 ('There shall come in the last days scoffers, walking after their own lusts'). Rochester, of course, walked at record-breaking speed after his own lusts, and Burnet thought him an inveterate scoffer:

> Upon this and some such Occasions, I told him, I saw the ill use he made of his Wit, by which he slurred the gravest things with a slight dash of his Fancy: and the pleasure he found in such wanton Expressions, as calling the doing of Miracles, *the shewing of a trick*, did really keep him from examining them, with that care which such things required.[22]

Even outright atheism seemed less of a threat than this gradual erosion of traditional pieties, this tiny insidious gesture, a slight dash of fancy. Premeditated sin had its own logic, an angling after reward or gratification. But scoffing seemed utterly unreasonable: wanton, extravagant, gratuitous. It short-circuited that modest examination of evidence on which Burnet and his colleagues had staked their careers, and the prosperity of England. It gave them no end of trouble.

For Rochester was not the only one. Stillingfleet, preaching before the King in 1667, claimed to see them everywhere. The

---

[22] In Farley-Hills, *Critical Heritage*, p. 69.

age, he protested morosely, is full of people whose manners are so bad 'that scarce any thing can be imagined worse, unless it be the wit they use to excuse them with. Such who take the measure of mans perfection downwards, and the nearer they approach to beasts, the more they think themselves to act like men.'[23] It became a persistent theme, of obvious relevance to the author of *Tunbridge Wells* and the *Satyr.* Joseph Glanvill soon followed Stillingfleet into the fray, issuing a series of zestfully paranoid sermons and pamphlets. Glanvill was convinced that the wits were conspiring to abuse and jeer at defenceless clergymen. The anonymous *Character of a Coffee-House, with the Symptomes of a Town-Wit*, published early in 1673, carries enough verbal echoes, and enough paranoia, to be his. It identifies the Town-Wit by his readiness to ridicule whatever is 'sacred or serious' and to 'abuse *Sacred Scripture*, make a mock of eternal Flames, Joque on the venerable Mysteries of Religion'.[24] Small wonder, then, that Rochester's prologue to *The Empress of Morocco*, a play first acted before Charles in the spring of the same year, should complain of the disrepute into which wit had recently fallen.

A year later Glanvill published, again anonymously, *An Apology and Advice for some of the Clergy, Who Suffer under False, and Scandalous Reports. Written on the Occasion of the Second Part of the Rehearsal Transpros'd.* He claimed that it was no longer enough for a clergyman to be entirely innocent, 'while there are any who have the ill-will to accuse them; and such there will be, while there are *Sects*, and Jovial *Atheists* in the world'.[25] Again, radical dissenters and idle gallants find themselves lumped together. According to Glanvill, such riff-raff combine to lampoon the clergy; and the charge they usually

[23] Stillingfleet, *Works*, I, 18.
[24] *Character of a Coffee-House*, p. 5.
[25] *Apology*, p. 4.

level is that of sexual misconduct. One 'jovial atheist' had just done this in *The Rehearsal Transpros'd*; another was ostentatiously applauding his wit, and repeating his jibes, in *Tunbridge Wells*. The battle-lines had been drawn plainly enough.

What appalled Glanvill was the hurtful gratuitousness of Marvell's insinuations. They seemed to give voice to a human energy which was impervious to reason. Like Rochester's libels or the habit of swearing, they could not be accounted for, let alone curbed. 'But what is it,' Stillingfleet enquired, 'which the person who despises Religion, and laughs at every thing that is serious, proposes to himself as the reason of what he does?' The scoffer, Tillotson agreed, 'serves the Devil for nought, and sins only for sins sake'; he risks the fires of hell 'for no other reward, but the slender reputation of seeming to say that wittily, which no wise man would say'. But people took such delight in mockery that there seemed to be no way of stopping them—they were, after all, conforming to the literary temper of the age. It is only too easy to mock religion, Tillotson thought, just as 'the most *noble* and *excellent Poem* may be debased and made vile, by being turned into *Burlesque*'.[26] The *Satyr against Reason and Mankind* is not a burlesque, but it does attempt to justify the burlesquing spirit of the age.

The condemnation of mankind in the first thirty lines of the poem is so generalized that it can only appear gratuitous, like the ending of *Tunbridge Wells*. It does no more than express a mood, however finely. The whole thing seems strangely detached, as much of an *ignis fatuus* as the eccentricities it complains about. Then Rochester remembers that there is a war going on. Wit has been identified in line 30 as a vanity and delusion. Now he sees the implications of this for a man whose role in society depends—to a considerable extent—on his wit.

---

[26] Stillingfleet, *Works*, I, 29; Tillotson, *Sermons*, pp. 117 and 87.

And suddenly, as if to clarify his real allegiance, he returns us to a concrete world where wits are kicked out of doors like prostitutes, and fops harbour a fierce hatred of those who have made fun of them. Enter a distinctly paranoid divine, determined to exploit this inadvertent disowning of wit:

> Then, by your favour, anything that's writ
> Against this gibing, jingling knack called wit
> Likes me abundantly . . .

The poem has begun to play up to a public controversy.

Glanvill's *Apology and Advice* had complained that if any clergyman

> be wont to reprehend the pretended *Wit*, and *Wits* of the Age, with spirit and smartness, . . . If he be sharp, and frequent in reproving and exposing the concomitant *Atheism*, and vile humour of deriding Religion and things Sacred; He then draws the *Railers*, and *Jesters* upon his back, who will . . . make him the constant mark of their malicious sport.[27]

Rochester's divine appears to covet a similar martyrdom:

> Perhaps my muse were fitter for this part,
> For I profess I can be very smart
> On wit, which I abhor with all my heart.
> I long to lash it in some sharp essay . . .

But the occasion for that has passed. Casual derision has been superseded by an even grander degeneracy: a railing attack on

---

[27] *Apology*, p. 4.

reason and mankind. The conflict between clergy and wits has moved onto a different level, and Rochester's divine adjusts to a new target.

The trouble with *Tunbridge Wells* was that nobody answered back. Its protagonist had railed in a vacuum. Only when the voice of piety answered back could invective develop from a mood into something approaching a political statement. Only then could one feel that all this ingenious scoffing had at least served to mobilize forces within society; that it might help to focus important social issues. Rochester wasn't exactly carried away by these grand opportunities. But he, too, changed the direction of his argument. He turned the tables on his adversaries by suggesting that it was not so much satire as reason and mankind themselves which must be considered gratuitous. Reason is 'impertinent' when not related to action (line 95), while human cruelty exceeds animal cruelty by its 'wantonness' (line 138). On the other hand, he could never quite purge the demon of wantonness from his own expressions, for the *Satyr* remains something of an insomniac's lament, perpetually exercising the very faculty it wishes to silence. And it certainly never achieved Dryden's aim of reproving without offending.

Stillingfleet, preaching before the King on 24 February 1675, fought back. It is very easy, he said, 'by ridiculous postures, and mimical gestures, and profane similitudes, to put so grave and modest a thing as *vertue* is out of Countenance, among those who are sure to laugh on the other side'. Furthermore, because it is impossible for these scoffers and mimics, when reproached,

> to defend their extravagant courses by *Reason*, the only way left for them is to make *Satyrical Invectives* against *Reason*; as though it were the most uncertain, foolish and

(I had almost said) *unreasonable* thing in the World: and yet they pretend to shew it in arguing against it: but it is pity such had not their wish, *to have been beasts rather than Men*, (if any men can make such a *wish* that have it not already) that they might have been less capable of doing mischief among mankind.

Satirical invectives against reason had escalated an already bitter dispute, as became obvious in 1676, when Glanvill published his *Seasonable Reflections and Discourses*. The wits, he said, mock believers '*for acting according to Reason*, that is, because they are *men* and not *bruits*: Because they act like *intelligent* Creatures, and not like the *Horse* and the *Mule* that *have no understanding*.' This seemed to him something of a last resort, since 'to deride men for governing themselves by their *reasons*, and not by *inferiour* principles, is as absurd, as if a man should laugh at the Ox for grazing freely in the field, and not standing still to grow like a tree'.[28] We don't know who Glanvill had in mind, because we can't say when the sermon was preached, although Evelyn heard him delivering another of the addresses in this volume at Whitehall on 28 February 1675. But it's clear that the jovial atheists had been concentrating their abuse on the faculty of reason, and had drawn an equally concentrated reply.

It may have been this reply which, in turn, provoked Rochester's 'epilogue'. For the last forty-eight lines of the *Satyr* represent another tightening from resonant generalities to immediate concerns, from mood to political statement. The court is now established, for the first time, as the scene of the action. It is here that the 'pretending part of the proud world' hangs out; and here that a churchman 'blown up with vain

[28] Stillingfleet, *Works*, I, 219 and 227; Glanvill, *Seasonable Reflections*, p. 41.

prelatic pride' reproaches the King and rails at men of sense. Stillingfleet, one might note, had been appointed chaplain-in-ordinary to Charles in 1667; Simon Patrick in 1671; Joseph Glanvill in 1672. The post, which enabled the incumbent to preach before the King, was held at various times by other latitude-men (Tillotson, Sprat, Burnet), and provided them with a very useful platform for their views. 'This is a season of tribulation,' Rochester wrote to Savile early in 1676, 'and I piously beg of Almighty God that the strict severity shown to one scandalous sin amongst us may expiate for all grievous calamities—so help them God whom it concerns!' Both modern editors think the 'strict severity' to be venereal disease.[29] But it is possible, I suppose, given the violence of the polemic against scoffing and the tendency to hold it responsible for all manner of grievous calamities, that the sin and the severity concerned were intellectual rather than physical. This might explain the studiedly lugubrious, holier-than-thou tone of the statement.

Circumstances, I think, shaped the *Satyr*. The poem demonstrates how an abstract sense of grievance can tighten into polemic, then lose political focus when the moment has passed, then tighten and clarify again. It was the specific challenge he had to meet which gave, and still gives, reason to Rochester's malice against reason. To put it another way, the *Satyr* shows how a paradox in the sense of an intellectual puzzle can become a paradox in the sense of a refusal of the accepted wisdom of the age. Like Artemisia, Rochester was pleased with the contradiction *and* the sin.

---

[29] *The Rochester-Savile Letters, 1671-1680,* ed. J.H. Wilson (1941); *The Letters of John Wilmot Earl of Rochester,* ed. Jeremy Treglown (1980). Text from the latter.

Libertinism and Sexual Politics

SARAH WINTLE

Rochester was a libertine. He is also often thought to have been an anti-feminist, and the two observations are connected. Seventeenth-century libertinism, with its emphasis on instinctive self-gratification and the pursuit of pleasure, inevitably involves certain attitudes towards women, some of which are brutally hostile.

> But they are ours as fruits are ours,
> He that but tasts, he that devours,
>   And he that leaves all, doth as well:
> Chang'd loves are but chang'd sorts of meat,
> And when hee hath the kernell eate,
>   Who doth not fling away the shell?

Donne's 'Community', even allowing for witty attitudinizing, is not one of his most sympathetic poems, but neither does it exhaust the range of possible libertine attitudes towards women. Libertinism indicates 'predilections of behaviour (rather) than an intellectual system',[1] and is therefore both various and

---

[1] Dale Underwood, *Etherege and the Seventeenth Century Comedy of Manners* (1957), p. 11.

intellectually self-contradictory. For example, the pursuit of pleasure through sexual variety can result in attitudes like that of Donne's poem, or equally logically but more subversively, lead to an attitude which grants rights of equal pleasure and promiscuity to women. Male libertinism in this last form then entails female libertinism, and this inevitably leads to the consideration of emotional, moral and social complications which the simpler attitude evades.

Some of these complications are raised, though obviously not from a libertine point of view, by Bishop Burnet in his account of his conversation with Rochester. Rochester himself appears somewhat ingenuous:

> . . . he told me that the two maxims of his morality then were that he should do nothing to the hurt of any other, or that might prejudice his own health; and he thought that all pleasure, when it did not interfere with these, was to be indulged as the gratification of our natural appetites. It seemed unreasonable to imagine these were put into a man only to be restrained, or curbed to such a narrowness: this he applied to the free use of wine and women.[2]

The use of metaphors of consumption seems characteristic of this particular libertine attitude. Rochester's use of such imagery in some of his poems is a great deal more subtle, and his exploration of the problems of male-female relationships in the context of libertinism often complicated and unorthodox. It is usually—though not always—too simple to call him an anti-feminist, and poetry seems to have forced him to confront problems that lurked underneath everyday prejudice.

[2] Gilbert Burnet, 'The Life and Death of John, Earl of Rochester', in *Lives* (1774), p. 18.

Libertinism, though, is not simply or exclusively concerned with the pursuit of pleasure. The libertine leant towards an intellectual scepticism, and he was particularly inclined to challenge the usual conceptions of nature and natural law, of society and social custom, and even the accepted ideas and practices of religious belief. This challenge to intellectual and social norms includes a challenge to the orthodox conception of woman and her status, even if these implications are not always spelt out. Rochester was not a particularly learned poet, but he was highly intelligent and able to seize upon and use the philosophical and conceptual commonplaces of his time and traditions. Besides, he had read a number of the major writers whose work contributed to the general body of ideas which make up Restoration libertinism.[3] Montaigne and Hobbes are of particular importance here, for both have interesting and even startling things to say about women.

Traditional non-poetic arguments for the subordination of woman to man can be briefly summed up in relation to the very areas of belief questioned by the libertines; there were arguments from the Bible—especially Genesis and the Pauline Epistles; arguments from nature; and, more elusively, arguments from social custom, inherited structures of feeling, and what might anachronistically be called a Burkean notion of prejudice. These arguments have been thoroughly explored elsewhere,[4] but a summing up is probably in order.

In what Ian Maclean calls the 'scholastic synthesis'—shaken and even modified by the Renaissance, but not broken up until the very end of the seventeenth century—arguments from the

[3] For an account of Rochester's reading see Dustin H. Griffin, *Satires Against Man: The Poems of Rochester* (1973), pp. 13ff.
[4] See Ian Maclean, *The Renaissance Notion of Woman* (1980) and Gerald Doherty, *The Renaissance Liberation of Women* (1972) PhD thesis, University of London.

Bible became inextricably mixed with arguments taken from an Aristotelian conception of nature.

> In the distinction of male and female may be discerned Aristotle's general tendency to produce dualities in which one element is superior and the other inferior. The male principle in nature is associated with active formative and perfective characteristics, while the female is passive, material and deprived, desiring the male in order to become complete. The duality male/female is therefore paralleled by the dualities active/passive, form/matter, act/potency, perfection/imperfection, completion/deprivation.[5]

This general picture was somewhat softened by Christianity and later by more particularly Protestant ideas of spiritual equality, and also by the influence of Florentine Neoplatonism. Nonetheless the basic paradigm remained deeply embedded in the European cultural heritage. Gerald Doherty, in his interesting and witty thesis *The Renaissance Liberation of Women,* suggests that the form/matter dichotomy was crucial, and that its withering away from popular consciousness under the influence of the new scientific and philosophical material-ism had a great deal to do with the enhanced status of women at the end of the seventeenth century.

In so far as this traditional paradigm did allow a positive view of women, the view was restricted and restricting. Women were allowed their virtues, but they were chiefly passive: 'long-suffering, humility, patience, compassion and public charity'.[6] Renaissance Neoplatonism undoubtedly enhanced women's status, but it, too, concentrated its praise in terms of the spirit

---

[5] Maclean, *Renaissance Notion of Woman,* p. 8.
[6] ibid., p. 20.

rather than the flesh. Woman, instead of being inferior because of her materiality, became superior because of her spirituality. Libertines like Rochester on the whole preferred their women to be substantial, not only for scientific and philosophical reasons; and materialism, in Rochester's case anyway, led to its own complications as far as the status or value of women was concerned.

Straightforward and socially acceptable Restoration views on women can be illustrated by two texts: an anonymously published handbook for aspiring gentlewomen, *The Ladies' Calling* (1673), and the better known and more aristocratic *Advice to a Daughter* (1688) by the Marquess of Halifax.

The Ladies' Calling is divided into two parts, with chapter headings as follows: I Of Modesty, Of Meekness, Of Compassion, Of Affability, Of Piety; II Of Virgins, Of Wives, and Of Widows. The epigraph is from Proverbs 31: 'Favor is deceitful and Beauty vain: but a Woman that feareth the Lord, she shall be praised'. The book is a good example of how old attitudes were modified but not substantially altered by seventeenth-century trends in religious thought.

In the informative preface the author plays with the idea that if women had the same education and upbringing as men, their intellects would prove equal:

And were we sure they would have ballast to their sales, have humility enough to poize them against the Vanity of Learning, I see not why they might not frequently be intrusted with it: for if they could be secured against this weed, doubtless the soil is rich enough to bear a good crop. But not to oppose a received opinion, let it be admitted that in respect of their intellects they are below men; yet sure in the sublimest part of humanity, they are their

equals; they have souls of as divine an Original, as endless
a Duration, and as capable of Infinit Beatitude.[7]

Ladies therefore should value themselves highly, and concentrate on cultivating their plentiful spiritual resources. Indeed,
in some respects, they have more advantages than men, who
being forced into the world are permanently tempted by
debauchery and excess.

> So that God seems in many particulars to have closelier
> fenced them [women] in, and not left them to those wider
> excursions, for which the customary liberties of the other
> sex afford a more open way.[8]

This is feminist writing of a sort, defining the pre-eminent
qualities of virgins, wives and widows, whose primary virtue is
modesty or chastity. Behind the book lurks the mirror image of
the modest lady, that literal perversion of nature, the woman
who is neither virgin nor wife nor widow but whore. Here, an
idea of woman is seen to be bound up with an idea of nature, and
a consequent idea of what is natural or right:

> An impudent woman is lookt on as a kind of monster; a
> thing diverted and distorted from its proper form . . .
> Certainly such are the Horrors and Shames that precede
> those first guilts, that they must commit a rape upon
> themselves (force their own reluctancies and aversions)
> before they can become willing prostitutes to others.[9]

Halifax's *Advice to a Daughter* is very different in tone,

---

[7] *The Ladies Calling* (1673), Preface.
[8] ibid.
[9] ibid., p. 14.

laconically tender and aristocratic, rather than pietist and middle class, but its ultimate assumptions and conceptual interweavings are similar, as the chapter forbiddingly entitled 'Husband' brings out, in a clearly political context:

> You must first lay it down for a foundation in general that there is inequality in the sexes, and that for the better economy of the world the men, who were to be the lawgivers, had the larger share of reason bestowed upon them; by which means your sex is the better prepared for the compliance that is necessary for the better performance of those duties which seem to be most properly assigned to it.[10]

Halifax slightly modifies this stark patriarchalism, first by admitting that women have emotional power over men, and then, presumably having read Milton, when he goes on to consider the possibility of divorce. He admits that some exceptional women might with justice plead to be free from their husband's dominion, but concludes that

> the law presumeth there would be so few found in this case who would have a sufficient right to such a privilege that it is safer some injustice should be connived at in a very few instances than to break into an establishment upon which the order of human society doth so much depend.
>
> You are therefore to make your best of what is settled by law and custom, and not vainly imagine that it will be changed for your sake.[11]

[10] Halifax, *Complete Works,* ed. J. P. Kenyon (1969), p. 277.
[11] ibid., p. 278.

Law, custom, and nature are here, in the Hookerian tradition, almost indissoluble.

Advice to a Daughter, written by the elder brother of Rochester's closest friend, was published in 1688, some eight years after Rochester's death. Its uncompromisingly patriarchal tone might remind us that it was at the beginning of the same decade, in the year of Rochester's death, that Sir Robert Filmer's *Patriarcha*, probably written as early as the 1630s, was first printed. Its publication was part of the political war over the Exclusion Bill, but nonetheless it has wider implications. Peter Laslett has argued that *Patriarcha* is important because it clearly articulates the prejudices and assumptions that underlay the social organization of the time, with its stress on 'the supremacy of the father, the inferiority of women, rules of primogeniture and so on'.[12] He sums up, 'Filmer for all his brash naivety and his obviously amateur outlook, was that extremely rare phenomenon—the codifier of conscious and unconscious prejudice.'[13] The Tory followers of Filmer and the moderate Halifax may have been poles apart politically, but their deepest assumptions about the ties of society, and those of most men of the seventeenth century, are not dissimilar.

Patriarcha may seem only indirectly relevant to the poetry of Rochester, but an idea of connection becomes clear when one looks at that extraordinary play by Nat Lee, *Lucius Junius Brutus*, first performed in 1680 and immediately suppressed for political reasons. The play is politically inflammatory in its mix of patriarchal republicanism, and psychologically peculiar in its father-fixation, but it has real dramatic and poetic power.

It tells of events leading up to the foundation of the Roman

[12] *Patriarcha and other Political Works of Robert Filmer,* ed. P. Laslett (1949), p. 22.
[13] ibid., p. 41.

Republic after the expulsion of Tarquin. One of Brutus's sons, Titus, is in love with Teraminta (acted, co-incidentally, by Rochester's ex-mistress Elizabeth Barry), an illegitimate daughter of Tarquin's. Titus supports his father politically, but Brutus's other son Tiberius backs Tarquin. Titus marries Teraminta but is forbidden by his father to consummate the marriage on the grounds that any contact with the Tarquins is polluting.

> Who would be there at such polluted rites
> But Goats, Baboons, some chatt'ring old Silenus
> Or Satyrs grinning at your slimy joys.[14]

Titus, forced to choose between his father and his wife, becomes a reluctant traitor through the machinations of Tiberius, but finally goes to his judicial death with a Roman spirit. Neither he nor his father will listen to the pleas of the women that sentiment and feeling should triumph over virtue and justice, and Titus dies happy in his father's arms.

Throughout the play, sexual dissoluteness, any emotional sympathy towards women, and political corruption are presented as closely linked. Brutus describes the debauched youth who follow Tarquin as

> Rome's Infamous and Execrable Youth,
> Foes to Religion and the Commonwealth,
> To Virtue, Learning and all sober Arts
> That bring renown and profit to Mankind;
> Such as had rather bleed beneath a Tyrant,

---

[14] Nat Lee, 'Lucius Junius Brutus' in *Works*, ed. T. B. Stroup and A. L. Cooke (1954/5), I, i, 213-15.

> To become dreadful to the Populace,
> To spread their Lusts and Dissoluteness round,
> Tho at the daily hazard of their lives;
> Than live at peace in a Free Government,
> Where every man is master of his own,
> Sole Lord at home, and Monarch of his House.[15]

The fundamental perception of this play seems to be that sexual and amorous indulgence of any sort leads to a kind of effeminacy, and thus threatens the fabric of the state, which depends on the establishment of social and moral male dominance.

There is an interesting comparison to be made between Lee's attitudes and a different kind of patriarchalism found in the Republican Henry Nevile's short piece of travel fiction *The Isle of Pines* (1668). The libertinism of Nevile's version of patriarchal politics might seem at first sight to be closer to Rochester's attitudes. Christopher Hill has pointed out similarities between the libertinism of aristocrats like Rochester and the radical free-thinking of way-out sectarians like Ranters. Hill describes *The Isle of Pines* as 'a cheerfully happy polygamous Utopia' which exemplifies the typical coexistence of sexual speculation and revolutionary politics.[16] The hero of the work, George Pine, enjoys on his desert island the services of four women, by whom he has altogether forty-seven children. The polygamy evidently continues generation unto generation because by the time Pine is eighty, he has 1,789 descendants—hence the book's title. Over these he appoints, as 'king and governor',[17] his eldest son, admittedly married to (among

---

[15] ibid., III, ii, 52-62.
[16] Christopher Hill, *The World Turned Upside Down* (1975), p. 314.
[17] Henry Nevile, 'The Isle of Pines', in *Shorter Novels: Jacobean and Restoration,* ed. P. Henderson (1930), II, 253.

others?) his eldest daughter. The whole story is an amusing example of what Gerald Doherty calls 'priapic fantasy'[18] in which sexual libertinism is uncomplicated because it is purely male and thus tied, one might add, to an undoubtedly patriarchal political system. Nevile sees women as unthreatening purveyors of both pleasure and offspring; Lee, with more profundity, sees that it is their very ability to provide pleasure that threatens the status quo, an insight, I shall argue, that Rochester shared.

Historians like Hill, Keith Thomas and Lawrence Stone[19] have pointed out that the political events of 1640-60 had a considerable and unsettling effect on women, on what they did, and what was thought about them. In the years of the Civil War and Interregnum, sexual freedom and experiment, though partly induced by the conditions of the war itself, were mainly associated with political beliefs of a radical kind, and such modes of behaviour and their implications—even if they were seen as a warning rather than a precedent—were not forgotten in the 1660s and 1670s. Equally, in the eyes of observers like Nat Lee, the goings on at the Restoration court threatened the patriarchal *gravitas* so necessary to a stable state. Rochester himself had been brought up virtually fatherless, and was later semi-adopted by the King. He may well have had ambivalent feelings about patriarchs, which would find echoes and counter-echoes in such a context.

It was not only the events of history which challenged traditional ideas. Two major thinkers, Hobbes and Montaigne, both of considerable influence on libertinism in general, were particularly radical in their approach to women.

[18] Doherty, *Renaissance Liberation of Women,* p. 118.
[19] Hill, *The World Turned Upside Down*; Keith Thomas, 'Women and Civil War Sects', *Past and Present,* 13 (1958), 42-62, and 'The Double Standard', *Journal of the History of Ideas,* 20 (1959), 195-216; Lawrence Stone, *The Family, Sex and Marriage In England 1500-1800* (1977).

Hobbes's ideas are obviously more straightforwardly political than Montaigne's. His remarks on the subject are brief, but their brevity did not hide them from the close attention of those scared or shocked by the general trends of his thinking. Bishop Bramhall, for example, was (from his point of view) rightly worried, seeing that Hobbes's principles 'destroy the subordination of a wife to her husband'.[20] The key text is chapter 20, book 2 of *Leviathan*. Hobbes argues here that paternal dominion is derived from the child's own consent, and not from the fact that parents beget the child. For if parenthood were the decisive factor, dominion would belong to both parents, and Hobbes thinks that this would be disastrous:

> And whenas some have attributed the Dominion to the Man only as being of the more excellent sex; they misreckon in it. For there is not always that difference of strength or prudence between the Man and the Woman, as that the right can be determined without War. In Common-wealths, this controversie is decided by the Civill Law; and for the most part (but not always) the sentence is in favour of the Father; because for the most part commonwealths have been erected by the Fathers, not by the Mothers of families.[21]

Hobbes goes on to consider what happens in the state of nature where there are no laws of marriage or of education, and ends by observing:

> If there be no contract, the Dominion is in the Mother, for in the condition of mere Nature, where there are no

---

[20] Quoted by Doherty, *Renaissance Liberation of Women*, p. 234.
[21] Thomas Hobbes, *Leviathan,* ed. C. P. Macpherson (1968), p. 253.

Matrimoniall lawes, it cannot be known who is the Father, unlesse it be declared by the Mother: and therefore the right of Dominion over the Child dependeth on her will, and is consequently hers.[22]

Such remarks throw out a lot of intellectual lumber and give a very real theoretical base for claiming woman's equality with man. Hobbes's atomistic individualism opens the way to an idea of woman as an autonomous being, rather than as inevitably dependent on and subordinate to man, as she is in the Aristotelian and patriarchal systems, which take the family rather than the individual as the basic social unit.

Montaigne's thoughts on sexual equality are mostly concentrated in the late essay 'On some Lines of Virgil'. The piece is typical of its author, in so far as it speculates in a subtle, radical and unfettered manner without ever drawing the revolutionary conclusions to which these speculations would seem to lead. At first, the discussion of the tedium of marital sex and the desirability of marriage based on the interests of fortune and family looks as though it is going to turn into the usual defence of double standards. But Montaigne moves on to a discussion of female sexuality, starting from the old anti-feminist jibe that women's sexual appetites are greater than men's. Accepting this, he points out the absurdity of enjoining chastity upon women as the supreme virtue:

There is no passion more exacting than this, which we expect them alone to resist, as being not simply an ordinary vice, but an abominable and accursed thing, and worse than irreligion and parricide; whilst we men at the same time yield to it without blame or reproach . . . we expect

[22] ibid., p. 254.

them to be healthy, robust, plump, well-nourished and
chaste at the same time; that is to say both hot and cold . . .[23]

and he then instances more examples of the hypocrisy of social
custom:

We train them from childhood in the service of love; their
charm, their dressing up, their knowledge, their language,
all their instruction have only this end in view. Their
governesses keep suggesting amorous ideas to them, though
always with the idea of exciting their disgust.[24]

He points out how men like to exaggerate the size of their sexual
organs through codpieces and in graffiti:

In short we lure and flesh them by every means; we
incessantly heat and excite their imaginations and then we
shout when we are hurt.[25]

The essay, like everything Montaigne wrote, is impossible to
summarize. It contains perceptive discussions of the poetic
language of love, jealousy, cuckoldry, sex as nature's joke, how
to behave during love affairs, all in the typical tone of generous
wry acceptance. The essay ends with a firm declaration:

I say that male and female are cast in the same mould;
saving education and habits, the difference is not great.
Plato, in his republic, invites all indiscriminately to share
all studies, exercises, charges and occupations, in peace and
war; and the philosopher Antisthenes rejected all distinc-

---

[23] Montaigne, *Essays*, trans. E. J. Trechmann (1927), II, 312.
[24] ibid., p. 313.
[25] ibid., p. 318.

tion between their virtues and ours. It is much easier to accuse one sex than to accuse the other; it is, in the words of the proverb, 'the poker calling the kettle black'.[26]

If Hobbes undermined the theoretical basis of patriarchy, Montaigne managed to look at the social determinants of female behaviour and status with an almost innocent eye. In the process, female sexuality is established as truly natural, with implications for religious doctrine and notions of law and custom which remain unexplored.

Partly because of the nature of the genres in which they write, Hobbes and Montaigne reach out towards generalization. This is particularly true of Hobbes, whose rational method attempts to provide a logical account of things as they really are. Montaigne's texts are calculatedly individual, prickly, inconsistent and open, but he often attempts, as in this essay, to make comments on the contemporary manners and practices of his society in general. Nonetheless, 'Upon Some Verses of Virgil' in its rather leisurely progress is full of inconsistencies or unresolved tensions, the most prominent of which is that between the idea that men and women are similar and even equal, and the idea that the pleasures and excitements of love rely on the sexes' fundamental oppositeness, their tendency to conflict and make difficulties for each other.

Rochester's lyrics, with their sense of dramatic situation, push towards the particular—this woman, this man. Their dramatic concreteness, often allied to formal precision, has the effect of bringing into prominence the inconsistencies and difficulties that Hobbes and Montaigne in their different ways gloss over. It is as if his poems are the experiments in which the more abstract or generalizing thinkers' hypotheses are put to the test or acted out. Sometimes the freedoms suggested come up against instinctive social prejudices and emotional habits instilled

[26] ibid., p. 358.

inevitably by the poet's upbringing and circumstances, and articulated as principles by the orthodoxly patriarchal writers on women's place in society. Sometimes the same freedoms are threatened by a darkly Hobbesian view of life as a constant battle between individuals for power over each other. Some of Rochester's most interesting love poetry oscillates between attempts to accommodate to an ethic of promiscuity and pleasure for both sexes—one logical outcome of libertine thinking—and the admitted and examined interference of other reactions, sometimes socially conditioned, sometimes inspired by hatred and aggression, sometimes by intense personal jealousy.

Lyric poetry had accumulated, by the mid seventeenth century, a whole collection of exemplary situations, conventions, *topoi* and tones for the analysis of the relationships of love. These obviously have a direct bearing on Rochester's poetry, with its roots in the Metaphysical and Cavalier writing of pre-Civil War days. But Rochester's poetry bears an oblique and complex relationship to the conventions and themes it uses, turning them upside-down and deflating them, sometimes with a certain viciousness. Thus both these older poetic conventions and the kinds of idea put forward by Montaigne and Hobbes are equally put to the test by the social and material particularity presented in poetry. Life as felt and life as codified and written about don't quite fit, and much of the power and interest of Rochester's poetry comes from exploiting this gap. Women are indubitably and awkwardly there, and preconceived strategies for accounting for and evaluating their behaviour won't do.

Rochester, though on occasion as capable of narrowly male fantasy as Donne or Nevile, is prepared in a number of poems to consider the implications of female sexual libertinism. This in itself is not new. One could instance a poem like Thomas Campion's 'A Secret Love or Two I must Confess',[27] where a

---

[27] Thomas Campion, *Works*, ed. Walter R. Davis (1969), p. 111.

wife argues that her secret unfaithfulness results in a sexual liveliness that can only benefit her husband. The joke here, though, is partly a variation on the old and boring theme of cuckoldry, and it is kept from being too nakedly shocking by the lyrical abstraction of the images used in the argument: 'The more a spring is drawn, the more it flows, / No lamp less light retains by lighting others,' and so on.

Cavalier verse and the kind of Restoration verse that descends from it developed a gentlemanly and high-handed way of dealing with the problem. This can be seen, nicely employed, in a song by Sedley which begins:

> *Phillis*, let's shun the common Fate,
> And let our love ne'er turn to Hate.
> I'll dote no longer than I can,
> Without being call'd a faithless Man.
> When we begin to want Discourse
> And Kindness seems to taste of Force
> As freely as we met we'll part
> Each one possest of their own Heart.

and ends

> Thus we will all the world excel
> In loving and in parting well.[28]

This triumphs through a carefully willed seemliness. These lovers will rationally refuse to be troubled either by social conventions of faithfulness or by irrational emotions like jealousy. Sedley does admit that the woman might tire of him first, and hints at a strategy for coping with the eventuality:

---

[28] Charles Sedley, *Poetical and Dramatic Works,* ed. V. de S. Pinto (1928), I, 6.

> If thy affection first decay
> I will the blame on Nature lay

but messy reality doesn't press very far into this poem. Its dramatic sharpness lies in the achievement of that very tone of voice which is designed to keep the messiness out.

Those lyric poems of Rochester's which contemplate female unfaithfulness or promiscuity are rather different. Take for example 'To a Lady in a Letter', which negotiates a kind of behavioural contract (one might think of *The Way of the World* here) between lover and mistress over the mutual toleration of different kinds of unfaithfulness — to bottle and to fop. Both he and she are true libertines; they both 'raise pleasure to the top', and indeed it is this lust for pleasure that constitutes her attractiveness:

> For did you love your pleasure less,
> You were no match for me.

The multiple meanings of 'match', all along the line from rivalry to contract, resound through this portrait of a libertine marriage. Pleasure, the basis of the relationship, is specific enough in this poem for Rochester to establish an equality which is not only spiritual and psychological, but physical too.

> Think not in this that I design
>   A treason 'gainst love's charms,
> When, following the god of wine,
>   I leave my Cloris' arms,
>
> Since you have that, for all your haste
>   (At which I'll ne'er repine),
> Will take its liquor off as fast
>   As I can take off mine.

The grotesque caricature of female sexual activity in these last two lines is funny enough, and appears to be being used as a jokily unstable analogy to excuse unfaithfulness—the poem generously gives to the lady the appearance of equal activity, though actually the reality of the metaphor is mostly on the man's side. But the poem contains rather more than rhetorical trickery. The speaker's unfaithfulness is to the bottle, not to a rival mistress, so the joke is to excuse another joke—or is it? Rochester did tell Savile he thought he was better at drinking than womanizing.[29]

The metaphor is the familiar one of consumption:

And when hee hath the kernell eate,
Who doth not fling away the shell?

Donne uses the idea as an image of psychological and social power; men use women as goods. Rochester, in the poem under discussion, makes the poem egalitarian: both sexes consume equally. In order to make them do this, however, in order to make the shift work, he is forced to take radical measures. In the interests of establishing physical equivalence between the two kinds of unfaithfulness the speaker turns himself into a parody of a woman. The paradigm of sexual activity in the poem is female rather than male.

Rochester's own bisexuality may be relevant here, but equally so, I think, is the tendency he shows again and again to a particularly reductive kind of materialism, which is as much a matter of the way his imagination worked as of intellectual convictions. This is nicely illustrated by a letter he wrote to his

---

[29] *The Letters of John Wilmot Earl of Rochester,* ed. Jeremy Treglown (1980), p. 67.

wife, spinning a burlesque scientific fantasy on the physiology of greatness:

> thence I inferr that as heate in the feete makes cold in the head, soe may it bee with probabilyty expected too, that greateness & meaness should bee as oppositely seated, & then a Heroick head is liker to bee ballanc't with an humble taile, besides reason, Experience has furnish'd mee with many Examples of this kinde, my Lady Morton nell Villers, & twenty others, whose honour was ever soe exessive in theire heads that they suffered a want of it in every other part . . .[30]

Doherty suggests that the influence of strictly philosophical materialism helped raise women's status.[31] Rochester, whose cast of mind seems to have forced him into a grotesque literalism on the subject, often found the implications more disturbingly complicated.

The poem returns to the central joke rather more crudely in its final stanza:

> Whilst I, my pleasure to pursue,
>   Whole nights am taking in
> The lusty juice of grapes, take you
>   The juice of lusty men.

This is unredeemed by caricature, and the physical equivalence as now pointed to has the paradoxical effect of establishing the lovers' separateness or apartness. Pleasure, mutual love of which is supposed to unite them, is actually seen as the solitary

---

[30] ibid., p. 75.
[31] Doherty, *Renaissance Liberation of Women,* p. 65.

activity of 'taking in'. Initial exhilaration in the equality or even the identity of the sexes leads, not to mutuality, but to a mechanistic, solipsistic sense of what pleasure really means under such circumstances. It is as if Montaigne's cautious optimism about sexual equality is found, when put to the test, to lead to a sardonically comic version of a Hobbesian nightmare.

Rochester's imagination was, it has often been remarked, deeply stirred by Hobbes's world. The classic instance of this is the lyric 'All my past life is mine no more' with its hopelessly atomistic view of time. He seems, too, to have been haunted by a view of sex as—if not brutish and short—at least solitary. 'Signior Dildo', although in the main a successfully frivolous squib, portrays a world where women can do without men altogether, for 'this Signior is sound, safe, ready, and dumb'—he provides pleasure with no risk, either of discovery or of entanglement. At the end of the poem, 'a rabble of pricks' try to get their revenge on Signior Dildo for his success:

> Nigh wearied out, the poor stranger did fly,
> And along the Pall Mall they followed full cry;
> The women, concerned, from every window
> Cried, 'Oh! for heaven's sake, save Signior Dildo!'

> The good Lady Sandys burst into a laughter
> To see how the ballocks came wobbling after,
> And had not their weight retarded the foe,
> Indeed 't had gone hard with Signior Dildo.

Signior Dildo's advantage lies in his emancipation from nature, from the reproductive weight of wobbling ballocks, from the vagaries of performance, and from ties of feeling. He is a sex machine and he allows women total independence of men.

Several other poems pursue this vision of mechanized solipsistic pleasure, without offering overt criticism. 'Fair Chloris in a pigsty lay' is another example, although it is a more complex and multivalent poem than the burlesque 'Signior Dildo'. It is an analysis of the social hypocrisy that could be seen to allow a girl pleasure as long as it is secret and involves no direct male activity. Montaigne's remarks on the way women are brought up to cultivate erotic fantasies in themselves and others, and yet forbidden to act the fantasies out, are pertinent here. Rochester, in allowing his readers to make this interpretation, also allows them to wonder if men are really necessary. Chloris doesn't need a man, only the idea of one. The point might be said to be undercut by the fact that the poem turns on the male fantasy that women long to be raped, but this is presented as fantasy within the poem itself. Self-administered pleasure is the final reality the poem leaves us with, a reality isolated and focused by the comically anti-pastoral romance setting.

Another related example is that strange poem 'The Fall', which envisages an Augustinian view of prelapsarian sex.

> Naked beneath cool shades they lay;
>   Enjoyment waited on desire;
> Each member did their wills obey,
>   Nor could a wish set pleasure higher.
>
> But we, poor slaves to hope and fear,
>   Are never of our joys secure;
> They lessen still as they draw near,
>   And none but dull delights endure.

Paradisal sex, like the delights provided by Signior Dildo, is entirely biddable, and to that extent mechanistic. Machines, unlike bodies, are 'secure'—security was the aim of Hobbes's great machine Leviathan—they do what you want and what you expect. In Paradise each sex uses the other equally, as an instrument for the satisfaction of desire and the provision of pleasure. Outside Paradise the human instrument is untrustworthy, and in this poem it is the lady who is thus, in a sense, the stronger.

> Then, Chloris, while I duly pay
>   The nobler tribute of my heart,
> Be not you so severe to say
>   You love me for the frailer part.

Rochester in this poem seems to see women's greater sexual strength as a result of the Fall. Either way, what one might call the political implications are grim. Sexual equality, even in Paradise, points to a bleak notion of contract: I use you, you use me. Otherwise, in a fallen world, the man can pretend to the nobler virtues of culture, but natural female dominance threatens.

Several of Rochester's poems portray sexually formidable women—'A Song of a Young Lady to Her Ancient Lover' and 'Upon His Leaving His Mistress' particularly come to mind. The women in both poems are related to an important figure in the development of libertine poetry, the Lucretian Venus, as I shall show. The Young Lady is able, through her physical powers, to bring her Ancient Lover back from the deadness of winter to the juvenescence of a second spring. It is this central idea as well as the charming refrain which has made the poem so popular, and so widely regarded as one of Rochester's most comically tender. But in fact its resonances are characteristically disturbing.

Doherty has pointed out that Carew's splendid poem *A*

Rapture celebrates the libertine liberation of woman in so far as it gives the woman a positive and active part in the lovemaking:

> My rudder with thy bold hand, like a tried
> And skilful pilot, thou shalt steer and guide
> My bark into love's channel, where it shall
> Dance, as the bounding waves do rise or fall.
> Then shall thy circling arm embrace and clip
> My willing body, and thy balmy lip
> Bathe me in juice of kisses, whose perfume
> Like a religious incense shall consume,
> And send up holy vapours to those pow'rs
> That bless our loves and crown our sportful hours,
> That wish such halcyon calmness fix our souls
> In steadfast peace, as no affright controls.

Rochester's Young Lady is too calculating and self-conscious to be as rapturous as this, but it is interesting to compare her sexual activeness with that of Carew's lady. Traditionally, and for obvious reasons—for example with Danae and the show of gold—the acts of bathing in juice or pouring have been seen as predominantly male, so here Carew, with his 'Bathe me in juice of kisses' is cleverly establishing mutuality. Rochester is less subtle, less delicately erotic, and in the second stanza his Young Lady takes over the male role almost completely:

> On thy withered lips and dry,
> Which like barren furrows lie,
> Brooding kisses I will pour
> Shall thy youthful [heat] restore
> (Such kind showers in autumn fall,
> And a second spring recall);
> > Nor from thee will ever part,
> > Ancient person of my heart.

The first two lines of this stanza are a reversal of an ancient and enduring image originating in *Timaeus*, where the male ploughs or fertilizes the female furrow, an image which parallels the Aristotelian distinction between passive female matter and active male form. Rochester here turns the traditional notion upside-down, rather than getting rid of it altogether. The Young Lady, too, has gone a considerable way towards taking over the male role by utilizing the same oral sexual analogy as operates in 'To a Lady in a Letter', albeit in rather a different way.

The one ancient thinker who did consider the idea of an active female principle was Lucretius, whose great nature-goddess Venus provides the primal energy of the universe. There is, however, a gap between Lucretius's metaphysical views about the goddess and his social views about her human avatars. Venus is a great active principle of fertility and creation; women are subject to sexual instinct but, although whores may indulge these instincts for the pleasure of men, respectable women are advised to remain sexually passive. They should remain still and experience no pleasure during the sexual act. The dichotomy between nature and society in Rochester's poem is less radical, but still quite marked. If one aspect of the young lady is Lucretian and Venereal, another is social and mannered:

> Thy nobler part which but to name
> In our sex would be counted shame . . .

It's hard to know quite how to take this. The need for purity of language is stressed by contemporary treatises on women. The author of *The Ladies' Calling* pays much attention to speech in his chapter on 'modesty', a quality which is opposed to 'boldness

and indecency' and which he defines as 'the science of decent
motion'. He adds that the ideal woman does not 'only refine the
language but tunes it too . . . a woman's tongue should indeed
be like the imaginary music of the spheres, sweet and charming,
but not to be heard at a distance'.[32] Chastity and linguistic
delicacy are near allied.

Whether the hypocrisy of the young lady in Rochester's
poem is knowing or not is hard to tell; if she *is* knowingly
hypocritical is she calmly accepting necessity, or being ironical?
A similar uncertainty can be seen in the lines:

> Yet still I love thee without art,
> Ancient person of my heart.

What is meant by art here? Her love is natural and instinctive;
it has to do purely with the giving of pleasure, not the
satisfaction of social demands and pressures. She doesn't employ
the traditional female arts to capture, or set snares. Yet this
doesn't seem quite adequate as an account of the poem, which
rather suggests that the young lady is indeed artful and skilled
in a possibly truer or more authentic version of love, having
studied with profit *Aretine's Postures* or *The School of Venus*.[33]
Behind even such a socially unconcerned and amusing poem as
this lies the perception that sexual behaviour cannot be
considered without suggesting its relationship to larger notions
of nature, society and art, and that these notions, revalued, can
alter our perception of the balance of power between the sexes.
Nat Lee, as we noted, saw the political implications of this, and
Montaigne, by redefining what women naturally were, also

[32] *The Ladies Calling*, p. 6.
[33] For an account of seventeenth century pornography see David Foxon, *Libertine Literature in England, 1660-1745* (1964), and Roger Fowler, *Unfit for Modest Ears* (1979).

pointed in the same direction. Like Montaigne, Rochester rarely comes to conclusions; that is not the function of poetry anyway. But it is part of the interest of much of his writing that it raises such questions, makes uncertain the status and meaning of such words as 'art' and 'shame', without offering any answers.

'Upon His Leaving His Mistress' is another poem that confronts a sexually formidable woman, and this time the pressure of feeling involved is much greater. Here the reaction to female inconstancy is jealous aggression, an instinctive assertion of an old emotional pattern that contradicts an intellectual commitment. It is worth turning in this connection to another, longer, poem, 'The Imperfect Enjoyment', which ends with a characteristically double-edged statement:

> And may ten thousand abler pricks agree
> To do wronged Corinna right for thee.

Ostensibly this is generous enough, putting things right for Corinna, deprived of her rightful pleasure because of her lover's premature ejaculation. But the second half of the poem has been a catalogue of projected obscene punishments for the offending member:

> Through all the town a common fucking post,
> On whom each whore relieves her tingling cunt
> As hogs on gates do rub themselves and grunt,
> Mayst thou to ravenous chancres be a prey,
> Or in consuming weepings waste away . . .

If the tone remains fairly constant between this and the final couplet, that final couplet expresses not only generosity, but also self-punishment, punishment not only of the prick but of the prick's owner. It is a kind of masochistic punishment through a freely contemplated jealousy, and it is a mark of the willed quality of that final generosity that this is what it has to overcome.

There is a similar feeling present in 'Upon His Leaving His Mistress', with its reversal of the conventional situation. Instead of the man wishing for variety rather than constancy for himself, he here gives his mistress over to the variety her 'merit' and 'inclination' call for. Yet behind this there is another scenario, a mirror image of the first—that of the lover leaving his mistress because of her unfaithfulness; this is a kind of extra-marital cuckoldry, a predicament no poet is likely to admit to straightforwardly. Thus the surface presentation can be read as a kind of philosophico-libertine cover-up which doesn't quite work. The poet's jealousy and consequent aggression are too intense.

However, if some of the unease in this rather interesting poem comes from semi-disguised jealousy, or jealousy half overcome through philosophy, that philosophy itself appears to be a second source of unease. Following libertine principles, generosity with the human body, a feature of the libertine's golden age, is natural and right, and paralleled in nature by teeming fertility and fruitfulness:

> See, the kind seed-receiving earth
> To every grain affords a birth.
> On her no showers unwelcome fall;
> Her willing womb retains 'em all.
> And shall my Celia be confined?
> No! Live up to thy mighty mind,
> And be the mistress of mankind.

This Lucretian Venus is in no way socialized, and dominant female sexuality is seen as terrifying. The poem leads on to

Rochester's more obviously anti-feminist pieces. The previous stanza, though, has involved a hint of the usual role reversal.

> Let meaner spirits of your sex
> With humbler aims their thoughts perplex,
> And boast if by their arts they can
> Contrive to make *one* happy man;
>   Whilst, moved by an impartial sense,
>   Favours like nature you dispense
>   With universal influence.

The words 'dispense' and 'influence' seem to be half returned to a primary physical meaning here, and the lady becomes an active giver rather than a terrifyingly passive devourer. She is a focus for a central ambivalence in the traditional process of sexual definition—as a powerful woman she is physically terrifying, so she has a masculine active power. Rochester's vision exposes the paradoxes and contradictions inherent in traditional methods of categorization. This is particularly clear if we read the poem, as I think we can, not as simply satirical, but as articulating a complicated and tense relationship between a vision of the logical possibilities of libertine sexual equality, and an instinctively orthodox reaction, compounded partly of fear and partly of socially inspired and aggressive ridicule.

Rochester's poetic contemplation of woman seems to have involved him quite frequently in showing how her nature could threaten the conventional categories of social discourse: nature/culture, male/female, individual/group, and finally and relatedly, the categories of class distinction. The poem in which these considerations are seen not perhaps at their most profound and exploratory but certainly at their most wide-ranging, is *A Ramble in St James Park.*

The role of jealousy in this poem is never in doubt; the

speaker is seething, and makes no attempt to overcome his feelings. The effort, rather, is to cultivate them and establish their rightness in a world where, horribly, sex is all. Once again, the libertine notion of variety of experience for all is confronted by the notion that some kinds of sexual activity are wrong, or rather, perhaps, nastier than others. Thus the poem both challenges some kinds of discrimination and attempts to establish others, though the old ones keep getting in the speaker's way.

Initially the park is presented as a place where all distinctions have broken down, and where promiscuity is as much social as sexual.

> Unto this all-sin-sheltering grove
> Whores of the bulk and the alcove,
> Great ladies, chambermaids, and drudges,
> The ragpicker, and heiress trudges.
> Carmen, divines, great lords, and tailors,
> Prentices, poets, pimps, and jailers,
> Footmen, fine fops do here arrive,
> And here promiscuously they swive.

The poet's distaste for this state of affairs ensures that some kind of categorization is bound to find its way back into the poem, and it soon does, through the unavoidable agency of the heart. Corinna, the speaker's mistress, should be different, but in fact she's the same as everybody else, and so, because of the distorting effect of feeling, worse. As he watches her go off with three witless and unattractive pretenders to social, intellectual and sexual distinction, the disgusted poet attempts to establish just what sexual freedoms he feels his mistress is entitled to.

Had she picked out, to rub her arse on,
Some stiff-pricked clown or well-hung parson,
Each job of whose spermatic sluice
Had filled her cunt with wholesome juice,
I the proceeding should have praised
In hope sh' had quenched a fire I raised.
Such natural freedoms are but just:
There's something generous in mere lust.

The point here about sexual unfaithfulness is that as long as it remains just sexual, it doesn't matter. As depicted at this point in the poem, it offers no real threat to the poet's ordering of things, to his sense of himself, either as a wit or as a sexual actor, an inflamer if not a satisfier of desire. Social inferiors are useful, like Signior Dildo, for providing extra pleasure at no cost.

This attitude is a vulnerable one, however, as we discover when, with masochistic intensity, the poet contemplates his mistress's adventure not with the rural clown or parson but with urban bully boys—porters and footmen—who fill her with 'nasty slime' rather than 'wholesome juice'. Dirt or nastiness, we have learned from the anthropologists, is matter out of place, and the concept is structurally related to ideas of social ordering. The country in this poem is there to serve the town, but urban civilization is continually threatened by a breakdown in its systems of discrimination. The poem opens with an urban parody of pastoral, and ends ironically with poet's curse on Corinna; that she should be

Loathed and despised, kicked out o' th' Town
Into some dirty hole alone,
To chew the cud of misery
And know she owes it all to me.

The 'natural freedoms' of natural lust depend, it seems, on a conception of natural order which is violated by the particular nature of the sexual and social promiscuities of Restoration London. Men could have affairs with lower class urban women, as we know Rochester himself did,[34] but for women the rules were different. There seems to have been some significant fascination, though, with the idea of women breaking those rules, exemplified in Rochester's scurrilous poem 'Quoth the Duchess of Cleveland to counsellor Knight' and in an episode in De Grammont's *Memoirs* where Lady Castlemaine is said to have had an affair with a rope-dancer or tumbler whose 'strength and agility . . . charmed in Publick, even to a curiosity of knowing what he was in private'.[35] Porters and footmen were free men, or at any rate in contractual employment; clowns and parsons had an older and more customary relationship to the aristocrats whose mistresses they (in the poem anyway) serviced. Something of the security of property and ownership would seem to be involved.

The three idiots, like the porters and the footmen, trespass from the realm of natural lust to threaten cultural order. Indeed they threaten the poet's and Corinna's status more precisely:

> But to turn damned abandoned jade
> When neither head nor tail persuade;
> To be a whore in understanding,
> A passive pot for fools to spend in!

The outrage is not only at Corinna's moral obtuseness, but that this obtuseness reflects badly on her lover and upon his ideas.

[34] Treglown, *Rochester's Letters*, p. 20.
[35] *The Life and Memoirs of Count Grammont* (1714), p. 110.

Ideally, natural libertine freedoms for both sexes and the right kind of social and intellectual distractions should go together: Corinna's action suggests that they don't, that the convenient separation of head and tail won't in the end work. An idea of freedom derived from a particular libertine notion of nature comes up against an altogether more anarchic and reductive notion of freedom, and behind the two ideas seem to lie, at an oblique angle perhaps, two views of social order. Corinna's action is truly challenging, and it is not jealousy alone that will account for the poet's rage.

A Ramble in St James's Park makes no statement; it triumphs through the energetic spontaneity of its abuse, through a kind of constructive incoherence. But in its mixture of intense personal feeling, and satiric and social observation, it too articulates, with what I have argued to be characteristic insight, the problematic implications of a considered female libertinism.

An Allusion to Horace

PAT ROGERS

The poem based on Horace's satire I. 10 has had its share of attention in recent years. It slithers in and out of the *Critical Heritage* volume, and it has been more extensively discussed in the past decade by Dustin H. Griffin, David Farley-Hills and others. There is also an important article by Howard Weinbrot.[1] I am in substantial agreement with the three critics named, for though they differ in some aspects of their reading they accord the poem roughly the same standing, and they have more shared assumptions than perhaps they acknowledge. All of them pay some attention to the link with the Horatian original, even if they describe this connection differently. For example, Farley-Hills argues that Rochester picks up the Dryden/Shadwell dispute 'by using Horace's poem to Dryden's disadvantage'. He goes on to suggest that the poem finally lacks conviction because the pose on Rochester's part is itself unconvincing—that is, the adoption of a 'role of Horatian arbiter of taste'. Weinbrot, like Griffin, notes some of the significant departures made in the later poem, and offers this statement of the general divergence: 'Horace gains our sympathy through association with a good man of letters;

---

[1] Howard Weinbrot, 'The *Allusion to Horace*: Rochester's Imitative Mode', *Studies in Philology*, 69 (1972), 348-68.

Rochester through disassociation from a bad man of letters.'
He contends that there is, directly, 'little thematic interplay
between the two poems', and speaks of Rochester's 'refusal to
be substantially in debt'. The attitude towards Horace is finally
neutral: the English satirist uses the Latin as a stalking-horse or
point of departure, not (as with Pope) as a constant reference
and moral gauge.

Much of this recent discussion seems to me to stand up well,
and I do not wish to pick quarrels here. Nor shall I attempt
anything comparable to Weinbrot's valuable consideration of
the meaning of an 'imitation' in the Restoration context. These
large-scale aerial views have their place in criticism, but it may
now be time to proceed to the immediate features of the
landscape.

The poem's very first phrase, for instance, points up an
important divergence from the model. Horace has 'Nempe
incomposito dixi pede currere versus / Lucili' ('To be sure, I
said that the verses of Lucilius run with a halting foot');
Rochester, 'Well Sir, 'tis granted, I said *Dryden's* Rhimes, /
Were stoln, unequal, nay, dull many times'.[2] Of course, Horace
is referring to a producible text and a particular occasion (the
fourth satire in this first book). Rochester, on the other hand,
hadn't to my knowledge said anything to the purpose in any
place, and certainly not in a parallel literary undertaking. So the
Latin word 'nempe' is supported by an authentic history of
previous discourse: the implied listener really would be able to
turn up the minutes to find the reference. Rochester has to
mount a greater feat of rhetoric, because there has been no real
situation to which the verbal gesture corresponds. The 'ongoing
dialogue' is a fabrication, and I think this shows: it sounds more
like the opening of a Donne satire than one of Horace's. From

[2] Quotations from Rochester's poetry are taken from the edition by V. de Sola
Pinto, *Poems by John Wilmot, Earl of Rochester* (2nd edn revised, 1964).

the start, then, there is something contrived or factitious about Rochester's strategy; but he doesn't care about that, as the Augustans might.

There is an interesting linguistic point at line 3. Rochester has 'What foolish *Patron* . . . so blindly partial.' This goes back to 'Lucili fautor inepte' in the original. (I think it is possible to speak of an original in this sort of case, where the earlier work is not so much paraphrased or developed as worked on, bounced off, so that it is, as it were, left intact by the imitation.) Now without the adverb 'inepte', the term 'fautor' in classical Latin merely meant a promoter or patron; the construction here suggests 'favens', meaning one applauding or protecting in a mindless sort of way. Translators usually import a bad sense by using an English word such as 'partisan'. But on the surface the expression is pretty neutral, and Rochester's 'Patron' is apt because that term itself had not slid very far into outright opprobrium, which it sometimes later was to indicate. It's worth recalling the first sentence of Johnson's *Dictionary* definition, as well as the follow-up, which is all we usually remember:

> *Patron.* One who countenances, supports or protects. Commonly a wretch who supports with insolence, and is paid with flattery.

What 'commonly' asserts is that you *could* support without insolence. In the present context it is certain that Rochester does wish us to have hostile feelings towards Mulgrave. But after all the drift is that Dryden gets the patron he deserves: and it's right that 'patron' shouldn't be an unremittingly hostile expression—that might deflect too much of the criticism away from the main object, Dryden.

In the following lines, there is something perhaps a shade

awkward in the management of tenses. Rochester speaks of Dryden's plays, 'embroider'd up and down' with wit, as having 'justly pleas'd the *Town*'. He then goes on to mention the 'heavy *Mass*, / That Stuffs up his loose *Volumes*'. Now plays are interesting because, even if they stay in the current repertoire, they tend to be identified with their first presentation on stage. As against Lucilius, available to Horace chiefly in terms of written works—*texts*, with their continuous present— Dryden is here first located by reference to dramas put on in the recent past. This is important, because it helps to elide one of the great differences in the subject-matter of the two poems. Lucilius is safely dead, a couple of generations back. Dryden is not merely alive, but, as we can now confirm with hindsight, not yet at his literary peak; he is still there in the argument. Horace has to face only the Lucilius party among contemporary critics; but at any moment Dryden may rise up and make his own contribution to the debate. This sense of a live opponent lends a certain menace to the *Allusion* which is highly characteristic of Rochester, and the sort of thing he turns to good poetic effect. One might point up the difference by saying that Horace is using a literary controversy with personal overtones, whilst Rochester is using a personal controversy with literary implications. But this would be going a little too far. The main issue is that past and present have different relations, and Rochester's sequence of tenses is coping with that fact.

I am aware that this is to simplify the cultural situation on both sides of the comparison. For example, in the case of Horace, Fraenkel makes it clear that the poet is taking sides 'in a struggle between rival literary parties . . . His place is on the side of Virgil, Varius, Asinius Pollio . . . and of all those associated with them. Horace is proud to belong to this circle; without overreaching himself (*haec ego ludo*) he knows that he has contributed and is contributing his proper share to the common effort.'[3] Fraenkel even speaks of the poem as 'the manifesto of an advancing force'. Similarly, in respect of Dryden, we must obviously read between the lines a subtext of implication which derives from Dryden's critical pronouncements. As Vieth points out, there is extensive reference, beginning at line 81, to the essay 'On the Dramatic Poetry of the Last Age', the more pointed because that essay makes significant use of this very satire by Horace.[4] Less directly, when words such as 'wit', 'fancy', 'spirit' and 'grace' crop up we may be invited to hear echoes of Dryden's own discussions of imaginative qualities, for example in his preface to *Annus Mirabilis,* with its touchstone of 'apt, significant, and sounding words'.[5] But the simplification is not very damaging if we hold on to the central distinction, which is that Rochester has the beast in view in a very real sense.

One surprising degree of literalism occurs at line 25, when Rochester advises the poet 'Your *Rethorick* with your *Poetry* unite'. The phrasing is obviously infected by the terms used by Horace: '. . . modo rhetoris atque poetae'. Are we meant to think primarily of *oratory,* as the Latin noun would direct us? Eighty years later, Johnson would define *Rhetorick* primarily as 'the act of speaking not merely with propriety, but with art and elegance' (the instances he uses being all taken from the post-Rochester period: Dryden, Locke and Thomas Baker). Only as a secondary sense do we get 'the power of persuasion, oratory', with examples from Shakespeare, Milton and Fairfax. Up to the middle of the seventeenth century, one would expect

[3] E. Fraenkel, *Horace* (1957), pp. 132-3.
[4] *The Complete Poems of John Wilmot, Earl of Rochester,* ed. David M. Vieth (1968), p. 124n.
[5] Dryden, *Of Dramatic Poesy and Other Critical Essays,* ed. G. Watson (1962), I, 98.

the latter sense to be the dominant one. Is Rochester importing some of the newer overtones, by a sort of pun on Horace's terminology? The *Oxford English Dictionary*'s sense 3: 'skill in or faculty of using eloquent or persuasive language' might be the nearest, but I leave this question to better scholars of the period.

Moving on to line 32, we encounter an interesting epithet, 'refined' Etherege. Of course, 'gentle George' was a friend and ally of Rochester. But if you stick closely to the order and logic of Horace's original, you could just place Etherege *after* the equivalents to the writers of old comedy (here, Shakespeare and Jonson) and *before* the aping and tedious Flatman. That would mean that Etherege corresponds to 'pulcher Hermogenes'. The Loeb translation[6] here has 'the fop Hermogenes'; it is true that 'pulcher' could mean excellent or noble, but the overtones of the translation seem right. Could there be any kind of covert allusion to Sir Fopling Flutter, who first appeared on the stage at the very juncture when (according to Vieth) the satire was written? Could there, that is, be a suggestion, however affectionate and oblique, of 'over-refined', 'too fastidiously elegant'? There is certainly some such element in Swift's use of 'refine', 'refined', 'refinement' a generation later.

Next, we come to a bit of evidence on the 'dog that did not bark' pattern. Rochester's decision not to supply a parallel to Horace's short autobiographical excursus can be explained by the different course his argument is taking around line 40 and following. He does not seem to have tried very hard to find an equivalent to Horace's reference to the mixture of Latin and Greek in Lucilius. Pope had no trouble in using French as an updated version of Greek in the *Epistle to Augustus* (line 263 and following). It is true that Dryden had not obliged by

---

[6] *Horace: Satires, Epistles and 'Ars Poetica'*, trans. H. R. Fairclough (1926, revised edn 1929), p. 117.

producing macaronic verse, but Rochester could have got round this. He evidently did not want to introduce too much by way of autobiography: it might reinforce the sense of a merely personal attack. As it is, Horace's charming conceit, lines 31-5 of the original, is simply lost.

The case for Rochester's 'un-Augustan' phrasing and outlook is supported in lines 69-70:

> Till the poor vanquish't *Maid* dissolves away,
> In *Dreams* all *Night*, in *Sighs*, and *Tears* all day.

A hard-line Augustan could scarcely have resisted the yawning opportunity for a chiasmus in the second line, either by recasting the line as 'All Night in *Dreams*, in *Sighs* and *Tears* all Day', or by revamping the couplet altogether:

> The melting Maid is vanquisht quite,
> By day in Sighs and Tears, in Dreams by night.

Not as good as Rochester, but it does show how easy it is to make the Augustan architecture spring up at command, and to get the emphases more pronounced.

I pass on to the culminating passage, that directly implicating Dryden. At line 75, Vieth simply notes: 'A "dry-bob" is coition without emission.' Certainly; but we are now so used to the obscene that we may not always realize when strong poetry takes the form of turning to obscene ends an innocent phrase. The point underlying Rohester's expression 'a dry bawdy bob' is that a familiar phrase is being travestied. A 'dry bob' had a more ordinary or at least more respectable meaning in the sense of 'a taunt, bitter jest, or jibe' (*OED*)— very common right through the seventeenth and eighteenth centuries. But *OED* also gives a more literal meaning, 'A blow that does not break the skin'.

This is surely much to the point. Dryden, though full of lubricity, is impotent, not just sexually but as a would-be damaging wit. To pursue the indelicate side of the phrase to the exclusion of all else is to miss an important part of the critique.

What then of the famous phrase 'Poet Squab'? I had always assumed this was a vague mode of abuse, based on the common sense of *squab* as 'short and plump'. But there seems to be more contemporary relevance in an alternative meaning, 'unfledged, raw, inexperienced'. That is how *OED* glosses the use by Shadwell in *The Medal of John Bayes*, and I think it must be applicable here too. The notion of Dryden in the middle 1670s as a callow youth may strike us as inapt, but the logic of lines 71-6 seems to rely on this idea of a green aspirant to the honours of Venus. Indeed, are not these lines very close in spirit to the famous story which Colley Cibber told of Pope— when the young man was 'slily seduced . . . to a certain House of Carnal Recreation, near the *Hay-Market* . . . [to] see what sort of Figure a Man of his Size, Sobriety, and Vigour (in Verse) would make, when the frail Fit of Love had got into him'? The 'little-tiny Manhood' of the poet is duly aroused, and Cibber righteously comes to the rescue of 'this little hasty Hero, like a terrible *Tom Tit*', when he is in danger of doing himself an irreparable injury.[7] One can surely detect in the passage by Rochester the scorn of a practised libertine for the bungling ineptitude of a piffling author attempting to turn urbane lover.

Lines 79-80 again have a lower autobiographical quotient. Rochester uses the image of a laurel distantly, dispassionately almost. Horace had said exactly the same thing in lines 48-9 of his satire, but in his case the remark follows on a small personal claim. What is in the English poet a mere gesture, a recognized figure of speech, has a real element of competitiveness in the

---

[7] *Pope: The Critical Heritage,* ed. John Barnard (1973), p. 337.

Latin. Rochester will not wrest the laurel, as a *post facto* claim;
Horace will not seek to wrest the laurel by his very practice, by
writing a poem in the precise vein pioneered by Lucilius.

At line 93 Rochester loses particularity and point, in limiting
himself to 'five hundred verses every morning writ': Horace is
not only more elegant but more comic in dividing the work into
sessions before and after dinner. The ending of this verse
paragraph is noteworthy because it endorses a mode of
composition which, we may think, conflicted with Rochester's
own practice, as compared with the ultra-correct Waller school:

> To write what may securely pass the *Test*,
> Of being well read over *Thrice* at least;
> Compare each *Phrase,* examine ev'ry *Line*,
> Weigh ev'ry *Word* and ev'ry *Thought* refine;
> Scorn all applause the vile *Rout* can bestow,
> And be content to please the few who know.

Farley-Hills might say this is unconvincing because it rests on
an urbanity Rochester seldom commands for long at a stretch.
Or, put slightly differently, that the message requires a poise
and certainty of tone which the medium resists. I am not sure
about this. One could surely argue that the absence of high
Augustan gloss gives the passage a sort of immediacy, of
catching the poet with the rubber end of his pencil at the ready.
There is occasionally something of a feeling of *de trop* when
poets like Horace and Pope call on us to blot our lines more
assiduously, because we know that some of their least-blotted
lines were already better than anything we shall ever achieve.
Rochester has a comforting degree not exactly of incompetence,
but of baldness: his technique only frays at the very edges, but
fray it does on occasion. His advice seems more *earned*,
consequently. One is always more inclined to take advice from

people who find it hard to obey their own injunctions, because they can have no vanity in promoting good practices to which they do not keep.

At line 111, Rochester introduces the figure of the courtesan Betty Morice. This enables him to get in a good Restoration riposte and convey something of the flavour of court life—a gain for his poem at this juncture. It is assuredly nowhere near as polished or deft as Horace's line and a half, where the resources of an inflectional language allow him to pack so much into the participle 'explosa':

> ut audax,
> contemptis aliis, explosa Arbuscula dixit.

('As the bold Arbuscula said, scornful of the rest [of the house], as they hissed her off.') 'Explodo' ('hoot off') was I suppose a good word in Latin, but it has become a better one in view of what has happened to the root in English. This is a supreme moment in the original satire, and whilst Rochester cannot match it he at least avoids disaster by the vivid anecdote.

One final difference, of course, is that Rochester omits the concluding farewell, and Horace's instructions to his boy to carry off his verses to add to his 'libellus'. A great deal is lost, for Horace does not merely round off his volume (something Rochester obviously couldn't do), but gets in a typical self-deprecating, yet purposeful remark. As we saw at the start, Horace is able to suggest that the present poem is a contribution to a larger whole—less, that is, of an off-the-cuff pronouncement. With Rochester, the finality has to be achieved internally, as it were, rather than externally. This is done through the powerful and resonant lines 120-4. He borrows 'I loathe the rabble' from another Horatian context in the *Odes* and makes a fine list of friends and admirers, all of whom seem to have good mouth-filling names. The concluding line lacks the brittle symmetry which an Augustan would have devised for it, but the point is made.

Now such hedge-hopping trips as this have their limitations. Yet within the existing accounts of the poem, it seems to me, there is a lot of detail to be filled in; and to study Rochester at close range is to come away with a realization that there is a great deal going on which has been overlooked in the broader controversies over his intellectual bearings and artistic identity.

In his fine book on Horace's satires, Niall Rudd observes that 'even if Lucilius and Horace had shared the same theories their temperaments would have led to different results'.[8] Yes: and their techniques, as well as their temperaments. Rochester is not merely writing in a different age from Horace, about a different target. He is writing in a different linguistic and critical context, for the triumph of the new 'Augustan' poetics was not in 1675 yet assured. One of the great merits of *An Allusion to Horace* is that it lives within seventeenth-century English as the original lived in the first-century Latin. What I have tried to do is show a few of the ways in which idiom bends in response to the needs of contemporary thought and feeling.

[8] N. Rudd, *The Satires of Horace* (1966), p. 117.

Rochester and Shadwell

RAMAN SELDEN

Several scholars have traced the complicated history of the theatre in the 1670s.[1] The rivalry between the King's Company and the Duke's had personal, commercial, political, and cultural dimensions, and the quarrel between Dryden and Shadwell was at least partly related to it. One of the more surprising changes of allegiance in the mid-1670s is that of Rochester, who, after having been on good terms with Dryden and the King's Company, suddenly, at the time when Dryden was meditating his devastating *Mac Flecknoe*, began to perceive virtues in the hitherto contemptible Shadwell. Rochester's poetic statements on Shadwell have been discussed before,[2] but not conclusively and not in relation to Shadwell's own dramatic development during the 1670s. David Vieth suggested that the realignment of Rochester's literary friendships, which apparently took place during the winter of 1675-76, 'probably originated in personal relationships'.[3] Without wishing to cast doubt on this

[1] See especially J. H. Wilson, *Mr Goodman the Player* (1964), chapter 3, 'The War of the Theatres'; A. Nicoll, *History of Restoration Drama 1660-1700,* (2nd edn, 1928), pp. 290-4.
[2] See J. H. Wilson, 'Rochester's "A Session of the Poets" ', *Review of English Studies,* 22 (1946), 109-16; D. M. Vieth, *Attribution in Restoration Poetry* (1963), pp. 303-4; K. E. Robinson, 'Rochester and Shadwell', *Notes and Queries,* 218 (1973), 177.
[3] *The Complete Poems of John Wilmot, Earl of Rochester,* ed. David M. Vieth (1968), p. xxix.

explanation, I would like to explore the literary significance of Rochester's changing attitude to Shadwell.

There is a passage in Graham Greene's biography of Rochester in which he suggests reasons for Rochester's dislike of Dryden. In passing he throws out this interesting comparison: 'Compare Dryden's fifteen hundred words of servility in *Marriage à la Mode* with Shadwell's dozen lines before *The Sullen Lovers*, which are like the friendly growl of a great dog in return for his bone.'[4] Greene here extrapolates from Rochester's views in *An Allusion to Horace* (1675/76), in which the 'heavy mass / That stuffs up' Dryden's 'loose volumes' is contrasted to the 'force of nature' at work in 'hasty' Shadwell's 'unfinished works'. However, in *Timon* (1674) Rochester had dismissed as insipid Shadwell's 'unassisted former scenes', an idea which is repeated later by Dryden in his lines on Shadwell's 'hungry Epsom prose'. It is evident from these two poems alone that Rochester's view of Shadwell either underwent a surprising change or was inconsistent. We know that Rochester's relationships with other dramatists of this period (Crowne, Lee and Otway) were fickle; in most cases there is no need to look for causes. His attitude to Shadwell was inconsistent and in this case, in my view, for good reasons.

We should begin by examining those passages in Rochester's poems which allude to Shadwell. It is best to consider *An Allusion to Horace* first, because it contains the only passage of overt praise, although even in this instance there is some ambivalence. It is worth keeping in mind the fact that there may have been as little as six months between Rochester's poem and the composition of *Mac Flecknoe.*

Rochester begins by casting Dryden in the unflattering role of Horace's predecessor Lucilius. The lines on Shadwell and Wycherley correspond to those in which Horace praises his

---

[4] Graham Greene, *Lord Rochester's Monkey* (1974), p. 177.

contemporary Fundanius, the comic dramatist. However, the details of Rochester's sketch of Shadwell are not borrowed from Horace:

> Shadwell's unfinished works do yet impart
> Great proofs of force of nature, none of art:
> With just, bold strokes he dashes here and there,
> Showing great mastery, with little care,
> And scorns to varnish his good touches o'er
> To make the fools and women praise 'em more.   (44-9)

'Ambivalence' may be the wrong word to describe the effect of these lines; and yet two possible readings suggest themselves. If we adopt a more orthodox Augustan viewpoint, we can produce the following argument: 'Shadwell's lack of artistic finish (a serious flaw) is partially redeemed by great touches of insight into human nature and manners. These strokes, however, are laid on with too little care and with a contempt for correctness and for those who expect it.' Another reading, and one which accords more fully with the text, suggests the following: 'Shadwell's great mastery of nature is enough to satisfy the audience; the lack of artistic finish is of no significance compared to the sheer boldness of his depiction of human nature. Only a fool would require the addition of an elegant surface.' Even this forces the sense of the phrases 'none of art' and 'with little care'; Rochester gives us no adequate rhetorical clue to judge the extent of their qualifying force. How serious a flaw is the absence of 'art' and 'care'?

Rochester's use of the Horatian model underlines the unorthodox direction of his thought about literature. Satire X, like the other 'programme' satires, emphasizes the artistic limitations of Lucilius and especially his lack of classical correctness: Horace speculates on the reasons which prevented his verses from being 'more finished and more smoothly flowing' ('magis factos et euntis mollius'). It is surely significant that Rochester not only omits to parallel these lines in his discussion of Dryden (he merely refers to 'those gross faults his choice pen does commit'), but actually excuses Shadwell's lack of finish, again following no hint in the Latin. As Vieth notes, 'hasty' Shadwell often boasted in his prefaces of his speed in composition. Rochester allows himself some inconsistency in attacking Dryden/Lucilius for this very fault:

> Five hundred verses every morning writ
> Proves you no more a poet than a wit.

Of course Shadwell's haste is redeemed by his 'bold strokes'. Rochester comes uncomfortably close to inverting Horace's aesthetics; after all, the Roman poet, while granting Lucilius natural vigour and satiric power, taxes him with serious artistic faults. Dryden regarded the *Allusion* as a perversion of the Latin original. In the preface to *All for Love*, he argues, in a thinly-veiled attack on Rochester, that writers of 'ignorant and vile imitations' who could 'make doggerel of his Latin, mistake his meaning, misapply his censures, and often contradict their own', were no friends of Horace and good poets.

Shadwell's prefaces in the years before Rochester's death display a striking negligence towards standards of design and correctness, an unconcern which incidentally casts light upon his relationship to his beloved Ben Jonson, whom Dryden called 'the pattern of elaborate writing'. In the preface to *The Sullen Lovers* (1668), his first play, Shadwell declares 'the want of design in the Play has been objected against me; which fault . . . I dare not absolutely deny . . . In Playes of Humour . . . there is yet less design to be expected', because 'humour' is 'pleasanter than intrigues could have been without it'.[5] Pepys's

---

[5] Thomas Shadwell, *Works,* ed. M. Summers (1927), I, 11.

first impressions of the play, before he succumbed to the charm of the 'little boy' who danced Pugenello,[6] tend towards Shadwell's own view: 'having many good humours in it, but the play is tedious, and no design at all in it'.

In the preface to *Psyche*, the operatic play damned by both Rochester and Dryden, Shadwell admits with a swagger, 'In a thing written in five weeks, as this was, there must needs be many Errors, which I desire true Criticks to pass by; and which perhaps I see myself, but having much bus'ness, and indulging my self with some pleasure too, I have not had leisure to mend them, nor would it indeed be worth the pains . . .'[7] He sums up his attitude in the Prologue:

> Five weeks begun and finish'd this design,
> In those few hours he snatch'd from Friends and Wine . . .

Finally, in the preface to *The Sullen Lovers* there is a passage which reminds one of Rochester's *Allusion* and which suggests why Rochester may have found Shadwell's careless approach attractive:

> Look upon it, as it really was, wrote in haste by a Young Writer, and you will easily pardon it . . . Nor can you expect a very Correct *Play*, under a Years pains at least, from the Wittiest Man of the Nation . . . Men of Quality, that write for their pleasure, will not trouble themselves with exactness in their *Playes*; and those, that write for profit, would find too little incouragement for so much paines as a correct *Play* could require.

Here we see what might unite a man of quality and a bourgeois dramatist. Rochester is certainly not an inexact writer, but

---

[6] Samuel Pepys, *Diary* 2 May and 4 May 1668.
[7] Shadwell, *Works,* II, 279.

neither was he a laboured one. Compared with Dryden, Shadwell may have seemed refreshingly unelaborate and natural to a writer who was often expressing himself in impromptus and lampoons.

The genuineness of Rochester's admiration for Shadwell in *An Allusion* is further suggested by his apparent use of Shadwell's Drybob, a conceited poet in *The Humorist* (1671), who prides himself on his 'wit' and 'Reperties'. There seems every reason to suppose that Drybob is a satire on Dryden;[8] Rochester's discussion of Dryden's feeble wit in terms of sexual defect ('a dry bawdy bob') seems to owe something not only to Drybob's name but perhaps also to Brisk's remarks ridiculing Drybob's pride in his power over the ladies: 'Oh impudence! Why sure you don't pretend to be a man fit for Ladies Conversation! What Charms have you to attract 'em?' Drybob replies: 'Is any man in *Europe* more notorious among Ladies, or valu'd for his pregnant parts, than Drybob?'[9] In *An Allusion* Sedley is admired for his ability to stir the fair sex 'with a resistless charm'; while 'Dryden in vain tried this nice way of wit'.

In May 1675, only a year and a half or so before the *Allusion*, Rochester wrote an Epilogue to *Love in the Dark*, in which he attacks the Duke's men on behalf of the King's men. His ridicule, here, of Shadwell's operatic version of *The Tempest* and the dramatic opera *Psyche* might appear to contradict the judgements in *An Allusion*. But while it is true that Rochester makes one or two unfavourable remarks about Shadwell as a writer, his main target of abuse is the meretricious staging and the showy witless acting. The audience's judgement is disarmed by 'songs and scenes', 'machines and a dull masque'. One can link this poem with a long tradition in Augustan satire and

[8] See M. W. Alssid, 'Shadwell's *Mac Flecknoe*', *Studies in English Literature,* 7 (1967), 396-7.
[9] Shadwell, *Works*, I, 245.

criticism descending through Horace, Ben Jonson, Dryden[10] and Pope, who all attack the excessive elaboration of stage business at the expense of verbal art and unity of design. And, even though in his first two plays Shadwell had introduced non-verbal entertainment, for obvious commercial motives (Pepys not only mentions the 'little boy' who danced Pugenello so delightfully in *The Sullen Lovers,* 1668, but also found the 'good martial dance of pikemen' the only thing to admire in *The Royal Shepherdess*, 1669),[11] he did not in fact take these theatrical diversions very seriously. In the prologue he declares rather mockingly,

> We've stuff'd in Dances, and we have Songs too
> As senceless, as were ever sung to you.

The preface to *Psyche* puts the commercial case quite unashamedly:

> Correcting the plays faults would not be worth the pains since there are so many splendid Objects in the Play, and such variety of Diversion, as will not give the Audience leave to mind the Writing; and I doubt not but the Candid Reader will forgive the faults, when he considers, that the great Design was to entertain the Town with variety of Musick, curious Dancing, splendid Scenes and Machines: And that I do not, nor ever did, intend to value my self upon the writing of this Play. For I had rather be Author of one Scene of Comedy, like some of Ben Jonson's, then of all the best Plays of this kind that have been, or ever shall be written.[12]

---

[10] See T. H. Towers, 'The Lineage of Shadwell: An Approach to *Mac Flecknoe*', *Studies in English Literature,* 3 (1963), 323-34.
[11] Pepys, *Diary* 25 February 1668/69.
[12] Shadwell, *Works*, II, 279.

Further light on Rochester's view of Shadwell is provided earlier, in 1674, in two brief but important allusions in *Timon* and in *Tunbridge Wells*. *Timon* is a poem in the Boileau tradition of the *repas ridicule*, with an opening scene descended from Horace's satire on the bore (I. 9). The allusion to Shadwell comes in these Horatian opening lines. The bore hands Timon a libel,

> Insipid as the praise of pious queens
> Or Shadwell's unassisted former scenes . . .   (15-16)

As Vieth points out, Shadwell was accused of having received the assistance of Sedley in *Epsom Wells* (1673). Rochester's couplet would appear to damn all Shadwell's work before then, but what of *Epsom Wells* itself? Without further evidence it would be impossible to decide whether Timon is implying that Shadwell's 'former scenes' are more insipid than his most recent work, or that *Epsom Wells*, having received the assistance of a fellow wit, hardly qualifies in any case for serious consideration. However, the first interpretation receives some support from the fact that in *Tunbridge Wells*, written around the same time, Rochester makes an allusion to Shadwell which is more substantial than has hitherto been recognized and which cannot easily be interpreted as hostile.

The passage in question (lines 114-48) concerns two barren wives who have come to the Wells to be made fertile. One recommends a husband for the other's daughter, who is suffering from retarded menstruation. The satirist comments:

> And ten to one but they themselves will try
> The same means to increase their family.
> Poor foolish fribble, who by subtlety
> Of midwife, truest friend to lechery,

Persuaded art to be at pains and charge
To give thy wife occasion to enlarge
Thy silly head! For here walk Cuff and Kick,
With brawny back and legs and potent prick,
Who more substantially will cure thy wife,
And on her half-dead womb bestow new life.
From these the waters got the reputation
Of good assistants unto generation.

Vieth notes the allusion to Shadwell's characters from *Epsom Wells*, Cuff and Kick, 'two cheating, sharking, cowardly Bullies', but fails to notice further extended references to the play. The key to the passage is the identification of 'Poor foolish fribble' with Mr Fribble, the 'surly cuckold' of Shadwell's play. Vieth, whose editorial practice is to remove initial capitals in substantives, prints 'fribble' with an initial lower case 'f', presumably interpreting 'fribble' as a common noun meaning 'trifler', a sense which ill suits the context. In Act II of the play, Mr Brisk declares 'Ay, Mr. Fribble maintains his wife like a Lady . . . and lets her take her pleasure at *Epsom* two months together'. Dorothy Fribble adds, 'Ay, that's because the Air's good to make one be with Child; and he longs mightily for a Child; and truly, Neighbour, I use all the means I can, since he is so desirous of one.'[13] In the opening scene of the play, Cuff and Kick refer to this aspect of the spa's reputation:

> *Cuff*: Others come hither to procure Conception.
> *Kick*: Ay, Pox, that's not from the Waters, but something that shall be nameless.

Later in the play Cuff cuckolds Fribble, who catches his wife in the act and has Cuff sent to jail. Fribble forgives his repentant

[13] ibid., 128.

wife, somewhat comforted by the prospect of four or five hundred pounds in damages from a jury of married men.

Rochester's version of the scene places greater emphasis upon the virility and potency of Cuff and Kick ('on her half-dead womb bestow new life'), but the passage cannot be regarded as an attack on Shadwell, or even as an implied criticism. It is true that Rochester overlooks Shadwell's moralistic conclusion, which he would no doubt have regarded as the sort of dull stuff that would have appealed to the London citizenry at the Duke's, the 'audience of substantial trades' satirized in the Epilogue to *Love in the Dark*. But the allusion to *Epsom Wells* is perhaps a tribute to Shadwell's naturalistic vigour—Rochester is able to overlook his bourgeois moralizing and to enjoy the low-life realism of his comic scenes.

In this respect Rochester differs from Butler, with whom he is otherwise closely related. Rochester's anti-bourgeois, anti-plebeian stance owes something to Butler's but, unlike the older poet, Rochester cannot remain a detached observer; his sympathy with the unaffected vigour of the lowest orders breaks in upon his aristocratic scepticism. The contempt for porter and groom in 'Love a woman? You're an ass!' is very different from the attitude in 'Quoth the Duchess of Cleveland', where the Duchess asks her adviser how she can obtain sexual gratification without harming her reputation. The reply includes some Butlerian touches of anti-plebeian scorn:

> 'To some cellar in Sodom Your Grace must retire
> Where porters with black-pots sit round a coal-fire;
> There open your case, and Your Grace cannot fail
> Of a dozen of pricks for a dozen of ale.'

The Duchess's rejoinder switches the poem's direction from aristocratic wit to a subversive disdain for hierarchy:

'For I'd rather be fucked by porters and carmen
Than thus be abused by Churchill and Jermyn.'

In *A Ramble in St James's Park*, too, 'porters' and 'footmen' are more acceptable rivals than the affected knights to whom Corinna succumbs.

In *Tunbridge Wells*, the misanthropic satirist aims most of his shafts at the affected gentry: Sir Nicholas Cully, the 'would-be wit', and the 'cadets'. Dorimant's assessment of Sir Fopling Flutter in *The Man of Mode* has a similar tone: 'How careful's nature in furnishing the world with necessary coxcombs!' Rochester's setting for the poem is a 'true medley' of people from all classes. In this context he gives us sketches of individuals who all are the characteristic affected fools of Restoration comedy, with the exception of Cuff and Kick. Without claiming that Rochester admired Shadwell's characters, one can at least say that he found them memorable, and assumed them to be sufficiently well known to his readers to be used as typical low-life gallants.

One other allusion by Rochester to Shadwell's writing occurs in 'On Poet Ninny', one of the satires on Sir Carr Scroope. Far from being merely a generalized name for a foolish poet, 'Ninny' alludes to the character of the same name in Shadwell's first play, *The Sullen Lovers*. Scroope is attacked as 'the vermin' who 'fain would sting',

And dost at once a sad example prove
Of harmless malice, and of hopeless love.

Scroope is 'a conceited ninny',

> The just reverse [counterpart] of Nokes, when he would
>   be
> Some mighty hero, and makes love like thee.

Shadwell's Ninny, 'A conceited Poet' acted by Nokes, courts
Emilia with heroic verses and foolishly believes that she is in
love with him. Unknowingly in competition with Woodcock,
'A Familiar loving Coxcombe', he disputes with his rival for the
use of a room at Oxford Kate's (the Cock in Bow Street), where
each believes he has an assignation with Emilia. They draw
swords, but the feeble poet immediately backs off. Even so,
Woodcock declares pathetically 'If you do kill me, I will declare
upon my Death-bed, That you had Malice in your heart, dear
heart'. Ninny replies 'Who I? . . . I Malice; do your worst: I am
better known then so: I am not so outrageous . . .'[14] Finally,
disappointed in love, Ninny asserts that 'hence forward instead
of Heroic Verse, hereafter I will shew all my power, and soul
and flame, and mettle in Lampoon, I durst have sworn she had
lov'd me.'[15] If one accepts Vieth's date of composition, early
1678 (identifying the poem as the one referred to in John
Verney's letter of 25 April 1678),[16] it is possible that Rochester
saw Shadwell's play when it was revived on 28 July 1677;[17] he
was certainly in London during that summer.[18]

It would be wrong to underplay the inconsistencies in
Rochester's response to Shadwell; his mixed view may be
explained by the changes in the dramatist's own work. In the
period up to 1676, Shadwell displays some virtuosity, working
through comedy of humours, pastoral romance, comedy of

[14] ibid., I, 85.
[15] ibid., 91.
[16] Vieth, *Attribution,* pp. 348-9.
[17] See *The London Stage,* ed. W. van Lennep (1960-68), I, 259.
[18] *Savile Correspondence,* ed. W. D. Cooper (1858), p. 58.

manners, opera, dramatic opera and heroic tragedy. The first two original plays (1668 and 1671) have a distinctly old-fashioned Jonsonian manner, which Rochester and others naturally saw as dully lacking the wit and repartee of modern comedy. In *Epsom Wells* (1673) he attempts a more fashionable and less overtly didactic comedy, combining wit and gallantry in the high-life plot and racy naturalism in the low-life plot. In *The Tempest* (1674) and *Psyche* (1675) Shadwell exploits his talents in pursue of commercial success, building upon his experience of dramatizing the pastoral romance, *The Royal Shepherdess* (1669). Rochester's scorn of the Duke's Company's extravaganzas of 1674 and early 1675 may have been replaced by admiration for *The Libertine*, Shadwell's version of the Don Juan story.

The Libertine was first produced in June 1675—the month when Rochester smashed the King's sundial, and about six months before the composition of *An Allusion*—and was played frequently to packed houses. The philosophy of the play's libertines has some general similarities to the views expressed in Rochester's *A Satyr against Reason and Mankind*, probably written in 1674. Don John and his fellows often put forward Hobbesian arguments to justify their flippant hedonism; their only guide is 'Infallible Nature':

> Nature gave us our Senses, which we please:
> Nor does our Reason war against our Sense.

Don John declares that 'there is no right or wrong, but what conduces to, or hinders pleasure'. Don Antonio believes 'we live in the life of Sense, which no fantastick thing, call'd Reason, shall controul'. Don Lopes caps this with 'My reason tells me, I must please my Sense'.[19] Shadwell's intentions are

---

[19] Shadwell, *Works,* III, 25, 26, 28.

overtly moralistic: he presents a darkly satiric portrait of a
sadistic libertine whose frantic career of lust and violence is
brought to an end by avenging devils and hell fire. There is
something of the relish of Marlowe's Barabas in the portrayal
of Don John. Rochester may have been impressed by Shadwell's
understanding of the sinister side of a fashionable sensational-
ism; 'The Postboy' (if by him) is his own account of the subject.
While it is true that Shadwell's moral purposes require that
Don John's libertine philosophy [20] is more crudely deterministic
than Rochester's in the *Satyr*, Rochester would surely have
responded to the unobscured energy of the play. Both in *Epsom
Wells* and *The Libertine*, Shadwell displays an unusual ability
to actualize the idea of Hobbesian man in all his coarse vitality.

That there should be some affinity between an aristocratic
court wit and a bourgeois moralist seems at first unlikely. But
Rochester's appreciation of Shadwell's astringent portraits of
the common people is less surprising when one remembers his
fondness for mingling with the ordinary citizens of London in
disguise as Dr Bendo or a tinker. His approach to Shadwell was
very selective, and characteristically subjective and unorthodox.
Casting him as one of the heroes of a Horatian poem has a
helpfully disorientating effect on a modern reader who is
searching too anxiously for more predictable patterns of literary
history.

[20] See T. B. Stroup, 'Shadwell's Use of Hobbes', *Studies in Philology,* 35 (1938),
405-32.

Contributors

BARBARA EVERETT is a Lecturer at Oxford University and a Senior Research Fellow of Somerville College. She is an editor and critic of Shakespeare and is at present working on *Othello*. Her other recent publications have been on Marvell, Milton, Henry James and T. S. Eliot.

BASIL GREENSLADE is a Senior Lecturer in English at University College London. He has a special interest in the relations between literature and politics in the seventeenth century, and has written on Walton, Hobbes, Clarendon and Halifax in the *Review of English Studies, Huntington Library Quarterly* and other journals.

PETER PORTER is a poet and reviewer of verse, at present the regular poetry critic of the *Observer*. He has been Writer-in-Residence at the Universities of Hull, Sydney and Edinburgh. He has published eight books of poems and a short selection of Martial's poetry in translation; his most recent publication is *English Subtitles* (1981).

PAT ROGERS is Professor of English at the University of Bristol. He has also taught at the Universities of Cambridge, London and Wales. His books include *Henry Fielding* (1979), *The Augustan Vision* (1974) and *Grub Street* (1972). He is currently working on Johnson and his circle and on a biography of Joshua Reynolds.

RAMAN SELDEN lectures at Durham University and was visiting Associate Professor at Cornell University in 1980. His publications include *English Verse Satire 1590-1765* (1978) and many articles on seventeenth-century poetry and literary theory. He collaborated with Professor Harold Brooks on the forthcoming *Poetical Works of John Oldham* and is at present writing a book on literary theory.

JEREMY TREGLOWN edited *The Letters of John Wilmot Earl of Rochester,* published by Basil Blackwell in 1980. Formerly a lecturer in English at Lincoln College, Oxford and University College London, he is now on the staff of the *Times Literary Supplement.* He is general editor of 'Plays in Performance', a series about theatre history, has contributed articles on poetry and drama to a number of academic journals, and writes regularly for the books pages of the *Sunday Times.*

DAVID TROTTER has been a Lecturer at University College London since 1977. His book *The Poetry of Abraham Cowley* was published in 1979. *The Making of the Reader,* a book on twentieth-century English, Irish and American poetry, is forthcoming.

JOHN WILDERS is the Dean of Graduates at Worcester College, Oxford. Among his publications are an edition of Samuel Butler's *Hudibras* and *The Lost Garden: A View of Shakespeare's English and Roman History Plays.* He is a governor of the Royal Shakespeare Theatre and literary consultant to the BBC Television Shakespeare series, and is currently writing critical introductions to all the plays for the BBC edition.

SARAH WINTLE lectures in English at University College London. She studied at the Warburg Institute, and is at present working on a book about literary portraits of Oliver Cromwell in the seventeenth century.

Index

193